WRITING FOR YOUR LIFE

Developing Functional Writing Skills

by

Bonnie L. Walker, Ph.D.

AGS®

American Guidance Service, Inc.

Circle Pines, MN 55014-1796

Editors:

Barbara Pokrinchak, Ed.D
Beryl D. Little, B.A.
Ella Westbrook, B.A.

Printed in the United States of America

ISBN 0-88671-961-5 (Previously ISBN 0-86601-639-2)

Order Number: 80392

A 0 9 8 7 6 5 4

Contents

Unit 1
The Writing Process

SPELLING COUNTS

Careful writers check their spelling. They correct any mistakes that they find.

Directions: Read the paragraph below. Check the spelling. Circle any misspelled words that you find.

Shoes

Their are shoes tooday for every ocassion. You can buy shoes especialy for runing or joging. You can buy shoes especially made for walking. Every sport has its own special shoe. There are bowling, golfing, basketball, and basball shoes in any atheletic store. With all the shoes around, the most poplar thing to do with shoes is still to take them off!

Directions: Write the correct spelling above each word that you circled. Use the words in the box.

athletic	jogging	running	especially	there
popular	baseball	occasion	today	

For You to Do:
1. Write the paragraph correctly on your own paper.
2. Choose a story in today's newspaper to read. Look for spelling mistakes. Circle any that you find.

SENTENCE SENSE

A sentence, as you know, is a group of words that express a complete idea. You can put more than one idea into a sentence. But nobody likes a sentence that just rambles on and on.

You show where a written sentence begins and ends by the punctuation.

Three Sentence Facts

A sentence begins with a word that is capitalized.

A sentence ends with a punctuation mark, such as a period or question mark.

A sentence does not end with a comma.

Directions:

- Read the words below to yourself or out loud.
- Decide where the sentences should begin and end.
- Copy the sentences on the lines below.
- Capitalize the first word of each sentence.
- Put a period or question mark at the end.

You can be a healthy person you are in control of your life you can eat healthy foods when you are tired, you can rest or sleep everyday you can take a walk or do some other exercise the choice of whether to smoke or not to smoke is yours perhaps most important of all, you can choose good friends doctors say that happy people are healthy people

ALIVE! SENTENCES!

A writer has a choice of words. Choose words that say exactly what you mean. Choose sentences that make your ideas come alive!

To Think About

Which sentence do you like better? Think about your reason.

- The dew fell softly during the night covering the entire yard.
- Dew fell quietly last night over the whole yard.

A. ***Directions:***
- Find a more colorful word for each dull word.
- Write the number of the matching word in the space.

Dull Words	More Colorful Words
1. nice	_____ A. laughable
2. big	_____ B. entertaining
3. pretty	_____ C. pleasant
4. interesting	_____ D. appealing
5. funny	_____ E. enormous

You can spice up dull sentences with more colorful words. Practice this skill in the exercises below.

B. ***Directions:***
- Replace each *underlined word or phrase* with more colorful or appropriate words.
- You may use the words in the box below or think of some of your own. Use a dictionary to check the meaning if necessary.

succulent	starving	repugnant	preferred
arrived	satisfying	vociferously	

When I <u>got</u> home from work last night, I was <u>very hungry</u>. What a shock to find that we were having <u>yucky</u> liver for dinner! I would have <u>picked</u> something <u>good</u> to eat, like a hamburger and french fries. Nevertheless, with nothing else to eat, and my stomach growling <u>loudly</u>, I forced myself. Surprisingly enough, it didn't taste half bad. I guess when you're hungry, almost anything tastes <u>good</u>.

WRITE IT OUT! CONTRACTIONS

> Dear Uncle Mac,
>
> I would like you and Aunt Ola to visit us this year over the holidays.

When something *contracts,* it shrinks. Words can contract.

When we talk, we often use "contracted words" called contractions. But, when we write, we should write out the full word.

A. *Directions:* Write the letter or letters that have been left out.

Example: I am I'm ___*a*___

1.	you are	you're	______	8.	should not	shouldn't	______
2.	they are	they're	______	9.	would not	wouldn't	______
3.	we are	we're	______	10.	cannot	can't	______
4.	I would	I'd	______	11.	do not	don't	______
5.	I will	I'll	______	12.	does not	doesn't	______
6.	it is	it's	______	13.	did not	didn't	______
7.	she will	she'll	______	14.	could not	couldn't	______

B. *Directions:* Write out each of these contractions.

Example: I'm ___*I am*___

1.	he's	______________	8.	they're	______________
2.	we've	______________	9.	they've	______________
3.	can't	______________	10.	shouldn't	______________
4.	don't	______________	11.	I'll	______________
5.	you're	______________	12.	it's	______________
6.	I'd	______________	13.	you've	______________
7.	she's	______________	14.	wouldn't	______________

WRITE IT OUT! ABBREVIATIONS

Shortened words are called *abbreviations*. We use abbreviations in certain situations when we write.

Measurements

1 in.	1 inch
three ft.	three feet
2 lbs.	two pounds
thirteen oz.	thirteen ounces

Titles

I saw *Dr.* Randolph yesterday.	Doctor
Did you see *Mrs.* Smith?	Mistress
His name is Sam Barns, *Jr.*	Junior
Gov. Lewis signed the bill.	Governor

Names of Days and Months

Mon.	Monday	Jan.	January	Aug.	August
Tues.	Tuesday	Feb.	February	Sept.	September
Wed.	Wednesday	Mar.	March	Oct.	October
Thurs.	Thursday	Apr.	April	Nov.	November
Fri.	Friday	May	May	Dec.	December
Sat.	Saturday	June	June		
Sun.	Sunday	July	July		

Directions: Rewrite the paragraph below. Write out abbreviations, except for titles before names.

Last Mon. Mrs. Cathy Young visited her dr. His name is Rufus Webster. She hadn't seen Dr. Webster since the previous Oct. "I think you've gained two lbs.," he said. Mrs. Young protested. "OK," he said. "It's one lb. and thirteen oz." "That's better," she said.

____

____

____

____

____

____

ABBREVIATIONS

Dates and Times

A.M. Ante meridiem (before noon) I left at 8 A.M.
P.M. Post meridiem (after noon) The meeting starts at 7:30 P.M.
A.D. anno Domini (Latin for "in the year of our Lord") A.D. 1985
B.C. before Christ 70 B.C.

Degrees from Colleges and Universities

B.A.	Bachelor of Arts	M.A.	Master of Arts
M.D.	Doctor of Medicine	Ph.D.	Doctor of Philosophy
A.A.	Associate of Arts	D.V.M.	Doctor of Veterinary Medicine
B.S.	Bachelor of Science		

A. ***Directions:*** Answer each question below.

1. Which came first? A.D. 1215 or 1700 B.C.? ____________________
2. What is the abbreviation for a veterinarian's degree? ____________
3. Is Francis Smith, M.D. a doctor of medicine? ____________
4. What is the abbreviation for three o'clock in the afternoon? ____________
5. What is a B.A. degree? ___________________________

Parts of Addresses and Directions

St.	Street	Ave.	Avenue	La.	Lane
Blvd.	Boulevard	Pk.	Park	Ct.	Court
Pl.	Place	Apt.	Apartment	N.	North
S.	South	E.	East	W.	West
NE	Northeast	NW	Northwest	SW	Southwest

B. ***Directions:*** Rewrite the addresses below. Write out each abbreviation.

1. 1214 N. Ellis Dr. ________________________________
2. 67 Park Ave., Apt. 3A ________________________________
3. 36 King Blvd., NE ________________________________
4. 3 Palmer Ct. ________________________________

C. ***Directions:*** Write the name of the state where you live. Then write its two-letter abbreviation.

My state is ______________________________. Its abbreviation is ____________.

UNIT 1 REVIEW: Proofread, Revise, Recopy

Words to Know:

Editing — The entire process of preparing the final copy of your writing. Editing includes proofreading, revising, and recopying.

Proofread — To read carefully, looking for mistakes.

Revise — To make changes.

Recopy — To write over, usually to improve a paper's appearance.

Directions:
- Edit the paragraph below.
- After making changes, recopy the revised paragraph.
- Find run-on sentences, capitalization, and spelling errors. Write out abbreviations, including contractions.
- Look back to the other pages in this unit. Use a dictionary as needed.

The Snowfall

How much snow is required for a major snowfall? What's a blizzard? It all depends on were you live, says Dr. Gamble. In Atlanta, GA, one in. is enough. In Minn. you'd need several ft. A blizzard is a snowstorm with high winds the wind blows the snows into huge piles called drifts. In a major blizzard, you'll probley have to search around for your car or fence. People talk about a major snowfall for years afterwards.

The Snowfall

Unit 2
Handwriting Basics

MARGINS

Words to Know:

Margin — The blank border around the edges of the page on the left and right and at the top and bottom.

Indent — To move the beginning of the paragraph in from the regular margin.

Directions: Measure the margins of this page and write your findings below.

Top __________ Left: __________

Bottom: __________ Right: __________

Directions:

- You are to copy the selection below on your own paper.
- First, see that your paper has the margins ruled.
- Leave a one-inch margin at the left side of the page.
- With your pencil, draw a $\frac{1}{2}$″ margin at the right side of the paper.
- Leave a margin of at least 1″ at the top and bottom of the paper.
- Indent each paragraph.

Larry Mason started his own business. He sells frozen pizzas. They are called half-bakes. As you may have guessed, they are partly baked and then frozen. Customers bring them home from the store and put them in their freezers. When they are ready, people put them in the oven and bake them about fifteen minutes. When Larry needs a vacation, he likes to go skiing. Every winter as soon as the first snow falls, he heads for the mountains. The more it snows, the happier Larry is. After he skis, Larry enjoys sitting in front of a roaring fire in the ski lodge. Larry says that his job and his hobby are a lot alike. They start out frozen but end up toasty warm.

NEATNESS COUNTS

Your handwriting tells something about you. Be sure to write so that other people can read your writing.

Form your letters carefully. Think of the space between writing lines as being divided into half.

Directions: Write the letters of the alphabet carefully.

A B C D E F G H I
J K L M N O P Q R
S T U V W X Y Z a b
c d e f g h i j k l m n
o p q r s t u v w x y z

There's an old saying: "Mind your p's and q's." A "p" looks very much like a "q." How are they different?

Directions: Copy the following exactly.

Charleston, West Virginia

BE LETTER PERFECT!

Be sure to cross your t's and dot your i's. Write exactly on the line.

Directions: Copy each word exactly as it is written.
Make every letter "perfect."
Be sure your "m" doesn't look like an "n."

1. Mom ________ 6. sweet ________
2. now ________ 7. country ________
3. where ________ 8. common ________
4. were ________ 9. Union ________
5. Alice ________ 10. music ________

Directions: Copy each sentence exactly as it is written.
Cross those t's! Dot those i's!

1. Jack drinks decaffeinated coffee.

____

2. Caffeine is found in tea.

____

3. We love the taste of sugar.

____

4. Fruits are naturally sweet.

____

5. Vegetables are naturally salty.

____

6. There's no better snack than raisins.

____

7. "You are what you eat!"

____

UNIT 2 REVIEW: Proofread, Revise, Recopy

Words to Know:

Proofread — To read carefully, looking for mistakes.

Revise — To make changes.

Recopy — To copy over, usually to improve a paper's appearance.

Directions:

- The paragraph below has been written sloppily.
- There are spelling and punctuation mistakes.
- Some sentences do not end with a period.
- The writer did not indent the paragraph.
- Your task is to proofread, revise, and recopy.

The First Day of Spring

In some areas the weather turnes cold in the winter. In those place people enjoy the furst day of spring verry much! .On that special day people wake up and look outside and see the sunshine they see blue skies they go outside to get the daily newspaper and feel the warmth in the air. Its trully a glorious feeling.

▶ Recopy the paragraph here.

Unit 3
Using Everyday Words

SPELLING WORDS CORRECTLY

A. ***Directions:*** Circle the word that is spelled correctly in each set of words below

Example: nessessary (necessary) nesessary necesary

1. all right	alright	allright	alrite
2. sceince	science	scince	scence
3. beleve	beleive	belive	believe
4. furend	frend	friend	freind
5. begining	beginning	beginiing	beganning

B. ***Directions:*** The boldface words in the paragraph are spelled wrong. Cross out each boldface word. Write the correct spelling above each word that is spelled wrong.

Example: We enjoy ~~**atheletic**~~ athletic events.

My new **computor** is fun to use. The whole **familly** likes it. We keep information about the checks we write on a disk. I particularly like it for **writting** letters. Cathy, my sister, **luves** the spelling checker. After she writes an essay, the computer searches for **mispelled** words. My little brother Jamie's **favorate** program is a game. He's always begging the rest of us to join him. That computer was a good investment.

CONTRACTIONS

Recipe for Contractions

Step 1: Take two words.
Step 2: Put them together and remove a vowel.
Step 3: Replace the missing letter or letters with an apostrophe.
Step 4: Presto! You've got a contraction!

Say these words out loud:

A. ***Directions:*** Write the contraction for each of the following phrases.

1. cannot ____________
2. will not ____________
3. did not ____________
4. I will ____________
5. I am ____________
6. she is ____________
7. we will ____________
8. who has ____________
9. could not ____________
10. must not ____________
11. does not ____________
12. would not ____________
13. should not ____________
14. I should ____________
15. it is ____________
16. he is ____________
17. we would ____________
18. I have ____________
19. you are ____________
20. she will ____________

B. ***Directions:*** Write out the complete phrase for each of these contractions.

Example: it's *it is*

1. he'd ____________
2. she's ____________
3. who's ____________
4. I'm ____________
5. we're ____________
6. won't ____________
7. you're ____________
8. we'd ____________
9. I've ____________
10. doesn't ____________

SHORTENED WORDS

Word to Know:

Abbreviation — A shortened form of a word.

We abbreviate words when we write to save time or space. In formal writing situations, we would ordinarily write out the whole word. Normally in speech, we say the whole word.

Formal: Hello, Reverend Brown

Very informal: Hi, Rev.

Correct:

Dear Rev. Brown:

Are you and your wife free for dinner next Friday evening?

Directions: Rewrite the following sentences. Write out all the abbreviated words. Use the words in the box below.

Example: *Jack is three ft. four in. tall.*

Jack is three feet four inches tall.

junior	ounces	February	veterinarian
page	pound	Thursday	automobile

1. Callie Herman is a jr. member of that law firm.

____

2. Jill Garman was born on Feb. 21.

____

3. We would like you to come to dinner next Thurs. evening.

____

4. Karl, can you drive the dog to the vet?

____

5. The kitten weighs one lb. and seven ozs.

____

6. My bookmark is between p. 34 and p. 35.

__________ ______________________________

7. Last week Sam bought a new auto.

____

ABBREVIATIONS IN ADDRESSES

Writing can be formal or informal.

- A business letter is formal.
- A quick note to a friend is informal.

Informal:	*Formal:*
Holly Powers	Miss Holly Powers
4105 W. Gerald St.	4105 West Gerald Street
Los Angeles, CA 90049	Los Angeles, California 90049

A. ***Directions:*** Write your own name and address in formal style with no abbreviations. Place a comma between the city and state.

Full name with title ______________________________

Street address ______________________________

City, state, ZIP Code ______________________________

B. ***Directions:*** Rewrite each of the addresses below.
Spell out abbreviations, except for titles.

1. Dr. Nancy Silvers ______________________________
   121 Van Ralston St. ______________________________
   Reading, MA 01867 ______________________________

2. Taylor & Wilson, Inc. ______________________________
   12 W. 1st Street, SE ______________________________
   Ocala, FL 32674 ______________________________

3. Mrs. Elle Eshbaugh ______________________________
   18 W. Hagerstown Dr. ______________________________
   Montgomery, Ala. 36110 ______________________________

SPECIAL ABBREVIATIONS

R.S.V.P. — At the end of an invitation, people often write the letters "R.S.V.P." They stand for the French phrase: *Respondez s'il vous plait*, or "Please respond."

If someone writes R.S.V.P., you should let them know whether or not you can accept their invitation.

C.P.A. — John Edwards is a C.P.A. That means he is a certified public accountant. He passed a state examination for accountants. The state certifies that John Edwards is a qualified accountant.

Correct: John Edwards, C.P.A.
Correct: John Edwards is a certified public accountant.

---

etc. — "Etc." is an abbreviation for the Latin phrase *et cetera*, which means "and so on." We use this abbreviation to indicate that our discussion includes the remaining items in a series, although we are not going to list them all.

Example: Grandfather Knott's farm had many animals, such as horses, pigs, sheep, etc.

Grandfather probably had chickens, dogs, geese, cows, and other animals typically found on a farm.

Organizations — Some organizations are known by their initials. In formal situations, write out the complete title. In a paper, write out the name once. Then use the initials with no periods.

Some Well-Known Organizations

IBM	International Business Machines
NBC	National Broadcasting Company
FCC	Federal Communications Commission
YMCA	Young Men's Christian Association
NATO	North Atlantic Treaty Organization

Directions: Use each of the following abbreviations in a sentence.

1. R.S.V.P. ____________________
2. etc. ____________________
3. C.P.A. ____________________
4. IBM ____________________
5. FCC ____________________
6. NBC ____________________

LAST NAME FIRST!

In everyday situations, we often need to write people's names.

Here are some common names:

Smith	Jones	Wilson	Brown	Stern	Owens
Jenkins	Walker	Rogers	Johnson	Jackson	Turner

A. *Directions:* Use a telephone book for this activity. Look through the book. Find twenty common last names. Write them on the lines.

1. ____________________ 11. ____________________
2. ____________________ 12. ____________________
3. ____________________ 13. ____________________
4. ____________________ 14. ____________________
5. ____________________ 15. ____________________
6. ____________________ 16. ____________________
7. ____________________ 17. ____________________
8. ____________________ 18. ____________________
9. ____________________ 19. ____________________
10. ____________________ 20. ____________________

B. *Directions:* Circle each last name in the paragraph below that is probably spelled wrong. Write it correctly above the misspelled name.

George Washinton was the first President of the United States. The next one was John Adems. He served four years. Next, there was Thomas Jeferson. After him was James Madeson. The fifth President was James Monrow.

FIRST NAME LAST!

First names, even common ones, can be spelled many ways.

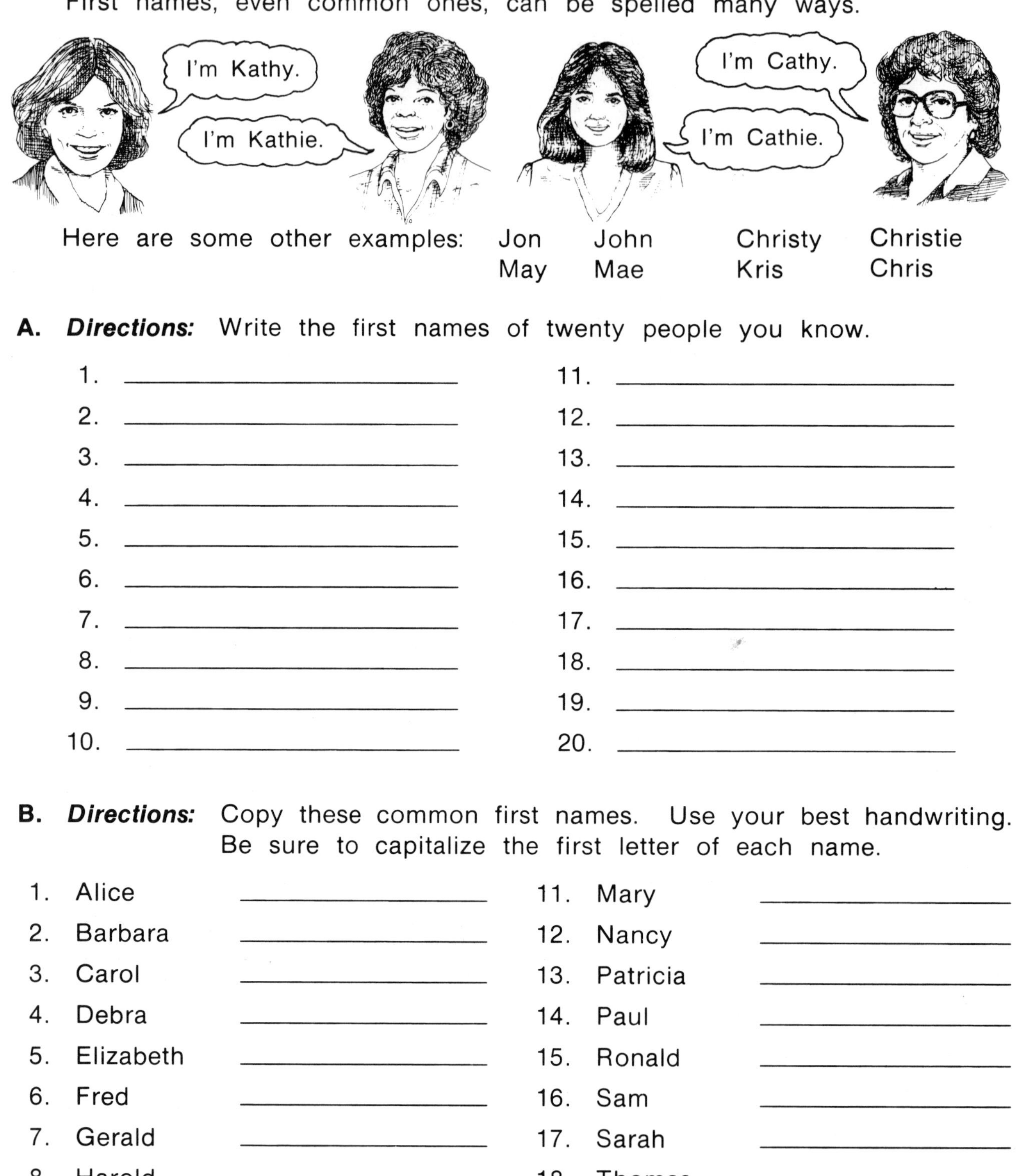

Here are some other examples: Jon John Christy Christie
May Mae Kris Chris

A. *Directions:* Write the first names of twenty people you know.

1.	______	11.	______
2.	______	12.	______
3.	______	13.	______
4.	______	14.	______
5.	______	15.	______
6.	______	16.	______
7.	______	17.	______
8.	______	18.	______
9.	______	19.	______
10.	______	20.	______

B. *Directions:* Copy these common first names. Use your best handwriting. Be sure to capitalize the first letter of each name.

1.	Alice	______	11.	Mary	______
2.	Barbara	______	12.	Nancy	______
3.	Carol	______	13.	Patricia	______
4.	Debra	______	14.	Paul	______
5.	Elizabeth	______	15.	Ronald	______
6.	Fred	______	16.	Sam	______
7.	Gerald	______	17.	Sarah	______
8.	Harold	______	18.	Thomas	______
9.	John	______	19.	William	______
10.	Laura	______	20.	Zeke	______

STREET ADDRESSES

Writing your street address correctly is very important.

We write an address like this: 14 Jonesboro Avenue, Apt. 12

Here are some names we give to roads:

Drive	Lane	Park	Parkway	Circle
Turn	Way	Street	Avenue	Boulevard
Road	Court	Highway	Route	Turnpike

Directions: Look up these words about roads in a dictionary. Write their meanings on your own paper. Use each of the words below in a sentence. Write the sentences on the lines provided below.

1. Drive ______________________

 ____

2. Turn ______________________

 ____

3. Highway ______________________

 ____

4. Route ______________________

 ____

5. Way ______________________

 ____

6. Park ______________________

 ____

7. Street ______________________

 ____

8. Boulevard ______________________

 ____

9. Turnpike ______________________

 ____

10. Road ______________________

 ____

CITY, STATE, AND ZIP CODE

An important part of your address is the name of the city and state, and ZIP Code.

A. ***Directions:*** Follow the directions to complete this exercise.

Mr. George Legare
12314 W. Westcott Turn
Pompano Beach, FL 33062

► Write the three abbreviations used in the address above. Then, write out each full word.

	Abbreviation	Full Word
1.	________________	________________
2.	________________	________________
3.	________________	________________

4. Write Mr. Legare's ZIP Code. ______________
5. Write your ZIP Code. ______________
6. Write the name of your state. ____________________

   Write its two-letter abbreviation. ________
7. Which one of these abbreviations is almost never written out? _____

   Circle your answer.

   A. FL B. W. C. Mr.
8. Which one of these abbreviations does not require a period? _____

   Circle your answer.

   A. DE. B. W. C. Mr.

B. ***Directions:*** Write out the complete word for each of these abbreviations.

9. Hwy. ____________________
10. Ave. ____________________
11. NE ____________________
12. SW ____________________
13. Mr. ____________________
14. Dr. ____________________

UNIT 3 REVIEW: Proofread, Revise, Recopy

A. ***Directions:*** Rewrite the paragraph below. Write the complete phrase for each contraction.

I'd like to invite you to a party. It's a celebration of my birthday. You don't need to bring a present. I'll be treating you!

B. ***Directions:*** Address this envelope to yourself. Use no abbreviations.

C. ***Directions:*** Write out the full names for these abbreviations. Use a dictionary if necessary.

1. FBI
2. AFL-CIO
3. UNICEF
4. UFO
5. UHF
6. P.O. Box

Unit 4
Working With Words

IMPROVING SPELLING SKILLS

To become a better speller, you need to practice these skills:

- Proofread your writing carefully.
- Learn to use apostrophes correctly.
- Identify vowels and consonants.
- Say words by syllable.
- Learn a few easy spelling rules.
- Recognize prefixes, suffixes, and root words.
- Check spelling in a dictionary.

A. *Directions:* Find five mistakes in the paragraphs below.
Rewrite the sentences. Correct the mistakes.

At the ocean on Friday, we saw several shipps passing by. They were on their way accross the sea. On ship was stoping at Le Havre, a port in France.

I am planing to take a trip to France someday. I think I'll like being a world traveler.

____

____

____

____

____

B. *Directions:* Write the letters of the alphabet that are called vowels.

____

Write your first name. ______________________

Circle all the vowels in your name.

RECOGNIZING INCORRECT SPELLING

Proofreading is the art of discovering words that are spelled wrong.

Here are a few proofreading tips to help you:

- Read the sentences out loud.
- Pronounce each syllable of "suspect" words.
- Pay special attention to words with apostrophes.
- Check contractions and possessives.
- Check for careless mistakes.
- Don't rush. Take your time.

Directions: Proofread the story below. Find ten spelling mistakes. Cross out the mistake. Write the correct answer above it. Do yours like the example below.

Like ~~meny~~ people, I love a parade! Years ago when I was a child, there were lots of parades. I remember especailly the day that World War II ended. It had been a long period of sacrafice for Americans. Many families were seperated. Now the sacrifice was over. Famalies would soon reunite. From inside my house, I heard music. Looking out the front window, I saw a group of peple marching by. Everyone was waving flags.

"Can I be in the parde, Mama?" I asked. I could see many of my friends already in line.

"Yes," she said.

I quikly ran out and got a flag. We all marched around the neighborhood cheerring all afternon.

APOSTROPHES: Possessives and Contra

1. Apostrophes take the place of missing letters.
2. Apostrophes show possession.
3. Apostrophes form plurals of letters, numbers, and signs.

Possessives:	**Mary's** hat	The hat of Mary
	The **clowns'** laughter	The laughter of the clowns
Contractions:	I **won't** go!	I will not go!
	Seven **o'clock**	Seven of the clock
Plurals:	I got 3 **A's**.	

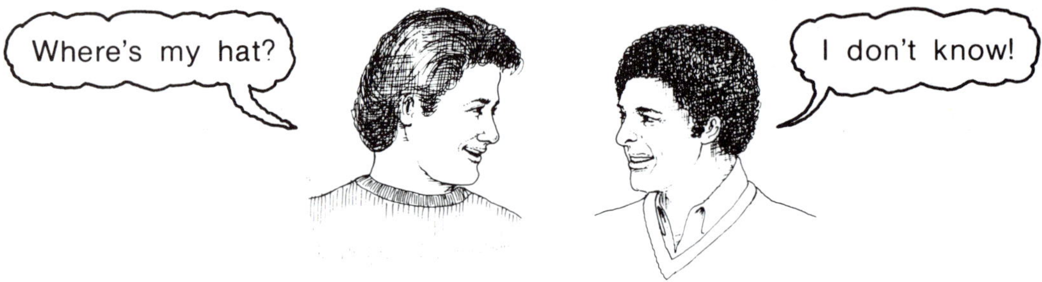

Directions: Read each sentence carefully. Identify each boldface word as a contraction, a possessive, or plural.

Examples:	Contraction	**I'll** be seeing you!
	Possessive	Did you see **Mom's** purse anywhere?
	Plural	I cannot get by **7's** when I play Jacks.

_______________ 1. **David's** gloves are missing.

_______________ 2. April **doesn't** like tomatoes that much.

_______________ 3. When you leave, please **don't** forget your hat.

_______________ 4. Number your answers by **2's**.

_______________ 5. "Mind your **p's** and **q's**," says Auntie Ethel.

_______________ 6. On the average, **men's** feet are larger than **women's**.

_______________ 7. Two of the most often used letters in English are **e's** and **s's**.

_______________ 8. **Peggy's** friends are coming over to watch TV.

_______________ 9. **Who's** that?

_______________ 10. The **teachers'** meeting lasted a long time.

VOWELS, CONSONANTS, AND SYLLABLES

To spell better, you need to be able to recognize syllables. A syllable is a word or part of a word pronounced with a single, uninterrupted sound.

Say these two words. Notice the difference. Circle the word that has more than one syllable.

catch	frozen

- The alphabet has two kinds of letters: vowels and consonants.
- The vowels are: a e i o u (sometimes *y*).
- All the rest are consonants.
- Every syllable has a vowel or vowel sound.

ch**ea**p — *ea* makes one sound.
d**o**ne — *o* is the vowel. The final *e* is silent.

A word may have many syllables, but each one has a vowel.

p**o**w**e**rf**u**l **pow • er • ful**

Directions: Rewrite each word below. Divide each word into syllables. Do yours like the example below.

Examples: community **com • mu • ni • ty**
grammar **gram • mar**

1. swimming ____________
2. skippy ____________
3. manual ____________
4. muggy ____________
5. comma ____________
6. magazine ____________
7. runner ____________
8. pencil ____________
9. computer ____________
10. dictionary ____________
11. swimmer ____________
12. Mary ____________
13. paper ____________
14. necklace ____________
15. power ____________
16. purple ____________
17. sharper ____________
18. mountain ____________
19. television ____________
20. record ____________

DOUBLING THE FINAL CONSONANT

Some spelling rules require you to identify vowels and consonants.

Sometimes we double the final consonant of a word before we add an ending. Sometimes the final consonant is not doubled. In this lesson, you will learn two rules that will help you to remember.

Look at these words: jog set log bat stop slip

These words have three things in common:

1. They are all one-syllable words.
2. They end with a single consonant.
3. There is one vowel before the final consonant.

Rule 1: When a one-syllable word ends in a single consonant, and there is one vowel before that consonant, double the consonant before adding an ending which begins with a vowel.

Directions:
- Rewrite each word listed below.
- Add the ending to the word.
- Double the final consonant only if the word follows the rule above.

Examples:

ship + ed	shipped	(double the final consonant)
sweet + ly	sweetly	(do not double the final consonant)

1. bat + er	______________	11. jump + ing	______________
2. toast + er	______________	12. top + ing	______________
3. play + ing	______________	13. slip + ery	______________
4. step + ed	______________	14. clear + ing	______________
5. fit + ed	______________	15. swim + er	______________
6. plan + ing	______________	16. cut + ing	______________
7. wrap + ed	______________	17. plant + ed	______________
8. hem + ed	______________	18. tap + ed	______________
9. hurt + ing	______________	19. drug + ist	______________
10. beg + ed	______________	20. run + ing	______________

WORDS WITH TWO SYLLABLES

Rule 2: When a word is accented on the last syllable, and it ends in a single consonant preceded by a single vowel, double the consonant before adding an ending which begins with a vowel.

Words Accented on the First Syllable		**Words Accented on the Second Syllable**	
signal + ed	signaled	begin + er	beginner
pilot + ing	piloting	forgot + en	forgotten
number + ed	numbered	control + ing	controlling

A. ***Directions:***
- Rewrite each word listed below.
- Add the ending to the word.
- Double the final consonant only if the word follows the rule above.

1. permit + ing ________________
2. admit + ed ________________
3. travel + er ________________
4. pilot + ed ________________
5. forget + ing ________________
6. equip + ed ________________
7. forget + ful ________________
8. differ + ence ________________
9. begin + ing ________________
10. signal + ing ________________

B. ***Directions:***
- Rewrite each word listed below.
- Add the ending to the word.
- Double the final consonant, if necessary.

1. shop + ing ________________
2. offer + ed ________________
3. nut + y ________________
4. bat + ing ________________
5. wonder + ful ________________
6. regret + ful ________________
7. teach + er ________________
8. sit + ing ________________
9. open + ing ________________
10. laugh + ing ________________

WORDS WITH A FINAL *E*

When a word ends with a silent *e*, you must make a decision before adding an ending. Do you keep the *e*, or do you drop it? Here are two rules that will help you.

Rule 1:	When words end with silent *e*, keep the *e* before adding an ending that begins with a consonant.

Examples: safe + ty = safety use + ful = useful

Rule 2:	When words end with a silent *e*, drop the *e* before adding an ending that begins with a vowel.

Examples: large + er = larger love + ing = loving

A. ***Directions:*** Practice using Rules 1 and 2. Write each word with its ending.

1. love + ly ______________
2. write + er ______________
3. care + ful ______________
4. hope + less ______________
5. lone + ly ______________
6. write + ing ______________
7. love + able ______________
8. care + ing ______________
9. hope + ed ______________
10. dive + ing ______________

B. ***Directions:*** Practice using Rules 1 and 2. Write each word with its ending.

1. practice + ing ______________
2. lone + ly ______________
3. compare + able ______________
4. use + less ______________
5. surprise + ing ______________
6. change + able ______________
7. age + ing ______________
8. circle + ing ______________
9. argue + ment ______________
10. chase + ing ______________
11. peace + able ______________
12. excite + ment ______________
13. believe + er ______________
14. waste + ed ______________
15. arrange + ment ______________
16. change + ing ______________
17. travel + ed ______________
18. advertise + ment ______________
19. voice + ed ______________
20. prove + ing ______________

I BEFORE *E*

Just remember this poem, which states the spelling rule.

I before *e*,
Except after *c*,
And when sounded as *a*,
As in *neighbor* and *weigh.*

Words with *ie*	Words with *cei*	Words with an *a* sound
chief friend	receive ceiling	neighbor weigh

There are a few exceptions:

science	weird	height
foreign	ancient	conscience
neither	either	leisure

Directions: Find the misspelled words in these paragraphs. Cross out each word that is spelled wrong. Write the correct spelling above the word. Use the rules and examples above.

science
Example: I believe that ~~sceince~~ is interesting.

To make a long story breif, my freind Janet got a new sliegh for her birthday. Not a sled, a sleigh. She shreiked for joy! "Although it's simply ancient," she told me, "my horse, Big Red, nieghed happily when he saw it."

Big Red has achieved stardom in our nieghborhood.

Janet's favorite liesure activity is riding around in the sliegh. Don't say this is wierd iether!

ROOT WORDS

A root word is a base word. You can often identify an unfamiliar word by first finding a root word within it.

Example: The root word *danger* can be found in **danger**ous and en**danger**ed.

Directions: Circle the root words in the left column. Then match the words to the meanings on the right.

A. 1. re(port) ____ a. to carry into
2. portable ____ b. able to be carried
3. transport __1__ c. to carry back, such as news
4. import ____ d. to carry or send abroad
5. export ____ e. to carry across

- What is the root word? ____________
- What does the root word mean? ____________

B. 1. dictate ____ a. to tell beforehand
2. contradict ____ b. manner of speaking
3. diction ____ c. to speak against
4. dictionary ____ d. to tell so that another may write down
5. predict ____ e. a reference book in which the words of a language are listed

- What is the root word? ____________
- What does the root word mean? ____________

Directions: Figure out the meaning of each of the following words.

1. If *bi* means "two," and *ped* means "foot," what is a biped?
____
2. If *pseudo* means "false," and *nym* means "name," what is a pseudonym? ____
3. If *psycho* means "mind," and *ology* means "the study of," what is psychology? ____

PREFIXES

Many words begin with prefixes. A prefix is a word part that is joined to the beginning of a root word.

Example: The prefix *pre* means "before."

Preheat means "to heat before using."

Directions: Match the words on the left with their meanings.

1. preview
2. prehistoric
3. prejudge
4. predict
5. preconceive
6. preface
7. precursor

____ a. To judge before you have all the evidence

____ b. A forerunner

____ c. An essay that comes before the main part of a book

____ d. To tell beforehand

____ e. To see before other people

____ f. Before historical records were kept

____ g. To form an opinion beforehand

The prefix *extra* means "outside, beyond."

Directions: Join the prefix *extra* to other words.
Write the meaning of each new word.

1. *Legal* means "according to the law."

   extra + legal ____________________

   Meaning: ____

2. *Ordinary* means "average, usual."

   extra + ordinary ____________________

   Meaning: ____

3. *Sensory* means "pertaining to the senses."

   extra + sensory ____________________

   Meaning: ____

NEGATIVE PREFIXES

Several prefixes mean "not" or "the opposite of."

Directions: Circle the prefixes in the left column. Then match the words with their meanings on the right.

A.

1. unpack	____	a.	safe
2. unnecessary	____	b.	closed
3. unopened	____	c.	take out
4. untrue	____	d.	not needed
5. unharmed	____	e.	false

- What is the prefix? ____________
- What does the prefix mean? ________________________

B.

1. incorrect	____	a.	not dependent on another
2. invisible	____	b.	not truthful
3. inactive	____	c.	faulty
4. insincere	____	d.	not active
5. independent	____	e.	not in sight

- What is the prefix? ____________
- What does the prefix mean? ________________________

C.

1. dishonesty	____	a.	to change the color of
2. discolor	____	b.	to regard as wrong
3. disorderly	____	c.	to feel no confidence in
4. disapprove	____	d.	not neat
5. distrust	____	e.	fraud

- What is the prefix? ____________
- What does the prefix mean? ________________________

SUFFIXES

A suffix is an ending that is joined to a root word.

Example: The suffix *-or* means "a person who does something."
An act**or** is a person who acts.

Directions: Circle the suffixes in the words at the left. Then match the words to their meanings at the right.

A. 1. caller ____ a. one who performs

2. believer ____ b. one who guards

3. actor ____ c. one who calls

4. sailor ____ d. one who runs a machine

5. protector ____ e. one who believes

6. typist ____ f. one who is easily excited or upset

7. alarmist ____ g. one who operates a typewriter

8. machinist ____ h. one who sails

- What are the suffixes? ____________________
- What do the suffixes mean? ______________________________

B. 1. greatness ____ a. state of well-being

2. kindness ____ b. that which shows a thought or feeling

3. happiness ____ c. state of enjoying anything

4. arrangement ____ d. act of directing

5. excitement ____ e. state of being much above average

6. enjoyment ____ f. state of being excited

7. direction ____ g. a kind act

8. expression ____ h. state of being arranged

- What are the suffixes? ____________________

MORE SUFFIXES

Some suffixes form adjectives.

Examples:

wash — *verb*	color — *noun*	self — *noun*
wash**able** — *adjective*	color**ful** — *adjective*	self**ish** — *adjective*
	color**less** — *adjective*	

A. *Directions:* Write the opposite of each word. Use *-ful* or *-less*.

1. hopeless ____________________
2. meaningful ____________________
3. careless ____________________
4. thoughtful ____________________

B. *Directions:* Circle the suffixes in the words at the right. Then match the words to their meanings on the left.

1. lovable	____	a. being at peace
2. peaceable	____	b. about thirty
3. audible	____	c. having style
4. stylish	____	d. able to be heard
5. thirtyish	____	e. worthy of love

C. *Suffix Practice.* Fill in the blanks with the correct words.

1. A new puppy can be ____________ to watch. (enjoyable, enjoyment)
2. Teenagers like to ____________. (sociology, socialize)
3. The company and the union came to a ____________ agreement. (peaceable, peacefulness)
4. The ____________ took a bow. (active, actor)
5. Leaves in the fall are ____________. (colorful, colorless)
6. Joe learned the most in ____________ class. (biologist, biology)
7. Fresh paint would ____________ this room. (beautiful, beautify)
8. To make a cake, follow these ____________. (directors, directions)

UNIT 4 REVIEW: Proofread, Revise, Recopy

Directions:
- Proofread this paragraph.
- There are spelling mistakes.
- Apostrophes have been left off.
- Rewrite the paragraph. Correct all the mistakes.

Wont you please come with me to the ice capades? The next show beginns at 8 oclock. Ive got two tickets. Some of the skatters are very powerrful. Im just a beginer myself, but I like to skate too. I use my friend Mary's skates since she outgrew them. Shes my nieghbor. I know youll like the skating show as much as I do.

Unit 5
Making Lists

FAVORITE THINGS

Making lists is one of our most common everyday writing tasks. In this unit you will practice making some lists.

Sample: **My Favorite Books**

1. Gone With the Wind, by Margaret Mitchell
2. The Accidental Tourist, by Anne Tyler
3. The Good Earth, by Pearl Buck

Rules for Titles: Capitalize the first word and all important words.
Underline titles of books.

Directions: Make a list of your five favorite movies.
Put quotation marks around titles of movies.

Example: *"Gone With the Wind"*

1. ______________________________
2. ______________________________
3. ______________________________
4. ______________________________
5. ______________________________

Directions: Make a list of your five favorite songs.
Name the persons who sang them.
Put quotation marks around titles of songs.

Example: "You Light Up My Life" by Debby Boone

1. ______________________________
2. ______________________________
3. ______________________________
4. ______________________________
5. ______________________________

SHOPPING FOR GROCERIES

Many people shop for groceries once a week. All during the week they write down things they need.

A. *Directions:* Make a grocery list using Monday's menus. Be sure to get everything you need.

Monday's Menus

Breakfast	*Lunch*	*Dinner*
eggs	cheese sandwich with mustard	tossed salad
bacon	pickles	green beans
cereal	carrot sticks	rice and butter
milk	milk	lamb chops
juice	apple sauce	hot tea with lemon
toast with butter		vanilla pudding

B. *Directions:* Imagine you were setting up your own apartment. Make a list of all the grocery items you might need.

Examples: soap, sugar, coffee

SHOPPING AT THE DRUGSTORE

Most people do some shopping at their local drugstore.

A. ***Directions:*** Make a list of at least ten items that you might buy at your drugstore.

Examples: toothpaste, magazine, film

1. ______________ 6. ______________
2. ______________ 7. ______________
3. ______________ 8. ______________
4. ______________ 9. ______________
5. ______________ 10. ______________

B. ***Directions:*** Here's Sam's shopping list.
Check the spelling of each word in a dictionary.
Copy the list over correctly.

1. flim ______________ 6. candie ______________
2. tissues ______________ 7. dog food ______________
3. magizine ______________ 8. envalopes ______________
4. vitimins ______________ 9. birthdya card ______________
5. asperin ______________ 10. scissors ______________

C. ***Directions:*** During the week, Bill writes down things to do. On Saturday he runs his errands and does shopping. Recopy Bill's list or make one of your own.

Pick up sodas and popcorn
Rent movie at the video store
Get oil changed in car
Take suit to dry cleaners
Pick up pizza for dinner
Return library books
Take dog to vet for shot
Shop for new shoes

Things To Do

____

____

____

____

____

A WEEK'S PLAN

Here's Sandy's list of things to do.

Monday:

- Do laundry
- Get milk at store
- Birthday card for Aunt Mary
- Call Jim
- Buy toothpaste
- Dentist appointment 3 P.M.

Directions: Try to think ahead.
Write down things you need to do this week.

Sunday:	**Monday:**	**Tuesday:**	**Wednesday:**
________	________	________	________
________	________	________	________
________	________	________	________
________	________	________	________
________	________	________	________
________	________	________	________
________	________	________	________

Thursday:	**Friday:**	**Saturday:**
________	________	________
________	________	________
________	________	________
________	________	________
________	________	________
________	________	________
________	________	________

PACKING FOR YOUR VACATION

When you go on a vacation, you pack a suitcase. You probably also put aside some other things to take.

Examples:

Books to read.

Games.

Address book.

A. *Directions:* Write all the things you'd want to pack in your suitcase.

______________________ ______________________

______________________ ______________________

______________________ ______________________

______________________ ______________________

______________________ ______________________

______________________ ______________________

______________________ ______________________

B. *Directions:* Write other things you'd like to take with you.

______________________ ______________________

______________________ ______________________

______________________ ______________________

______________________ ______________________

______________________ ______________________

______________________ ______________________

PLANNING A PARTY

A. *Directions:* Write the names of at least ten people that you'd like to invite to your party.

B. *Directions:* Write your shopping list for your party.
Don't forget napkins!

HOMEWORK AND OTHER PROJECTS

Making lists will help you keep track of school work. Write down:

- homework assignments,
- long term projects, and
- other things to do.

Here's Maureen's list:

- *Math — Page 45, Problems 1-15*
- *English, read Chapters 1-3 in Tale of Two Cities.*
  Answer questions at end of each chapter.
- *Study for quiz in English tomorrow.*
- *Write up science experiment.*
- *Science Club Tonight! Election of officers.*
- *Work on term paper, due next week, at library.*

Directions: Write your own list of things to do today. Then write your list of things to do this week.

Things to do today:	**Things to do this week:**

UNIT 5 REVIEW: Proofread, Revise, Recopy

A. *Directions:* • Make a list of your five favorite TV shows.
• Use quotation marks around the titles.

Example: "I Love Lucy"

1. ______________________________
2. ______________________________
3. ______________________________
4. ______________________________
5. ______________________________

B. *Directions:* Copy Jack's list carefully. Spell all the words correctly.

Jack's list:	*Your copy:*
My Favorite Desserts	____________________
• Chocolate fudge brownies	____________________
• Lemon meringue pie	____________________
• Chocolate chip cookies	____________________
• Strawberry mousse	____________________
• Cherry pie and ice cream	____________________

C. *Directions:* Just for fun, make a list of everything you would do or buy if you suddenly became a millionaire.

1. ______________________________
2. ______________________________
3. ______________________________
4. ______________________________
5. ______________________________
6. ______________________________
7. ______________________________

Unit 6
Sorting

PUTTING THINGS IN ORDER

Nearly everything we do requires us to put things in order. For example, we sort our clothes into piles.

Jack's

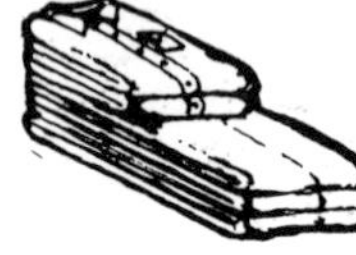

Dad's

Mom's

Tina's

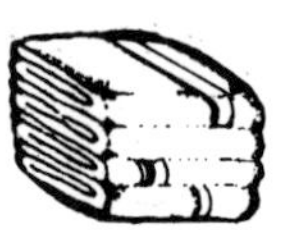

Towels

In an office people put papers in order in file cabinets. Usually folders are put in alphabetical order.

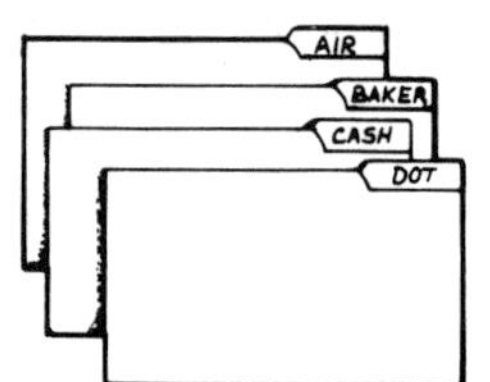

In a library, the books are put in order.

Fiction books are arranged according to the last name of the writer.

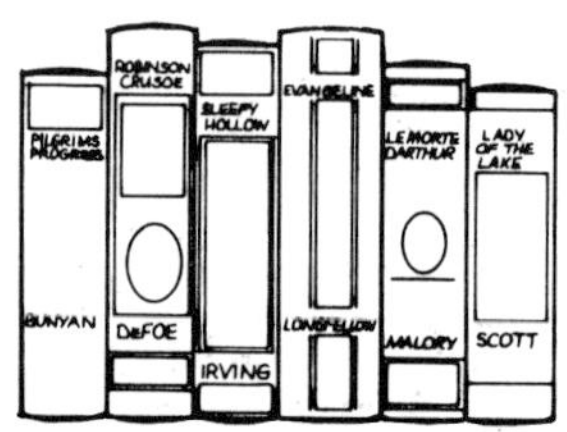

Nonfiction books are put in groups according to subject.

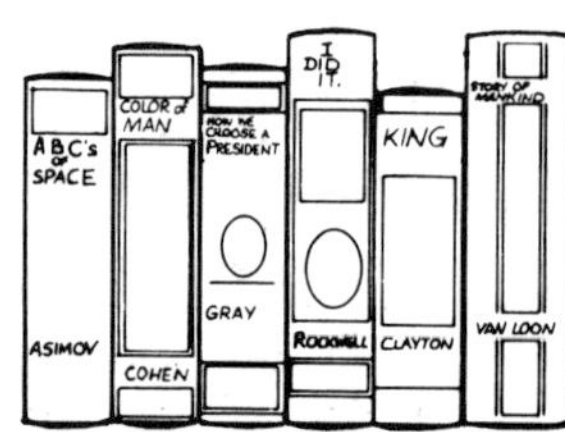

Directions: There are many ways to put things in order. Name as many ways as you can.

____

____

____

____

____

____

RULES OF ORDER

Here are the two most common ways to put things into order.

- Alphabetical (ABC order)
- Chronological (According to time, or date)

Practice 1: Arrange the words in each list in alphabetical order. Try to work as fast as you can. Do one list at a time.

Jack	________________	English	________________
Richard	________________	French	________________
Allen	________________	Chinese	________________
Fred	________________	Russian	________________
George	________________	Polish	________________

Practice 2: Arrange the numbers in each list in chronological order. Try to work as fast as you can. Do one list at a time.

May 8, 1983	________________	1152	________________
January 3, 1983	________________	2012	________________
April 1, 1981	________________	897	________________
August 22, 1980	________________	1401	________________
July 17, 1979	________________	1939	________________

Directions: Arrange these books in order three ways.

- Alphabetical by title
- By date
- By length — shortest to longest

	Title	Author	Date	Pages
1.	*Huckleberry Finn*	Mark Twain	1918	374
2.	*Watership Down*	Richard Adams	1972	429
3.	*Penrod*	Booth Tarkington	1914	306
4.	*Lake Wobegon Days*	Garrison Keillor	1985	337
5.	*Gone With the Wind*	Margaret Mitchell	1936	1037

Alphabetical by Title	By Date Published (first to last)	By Length (shortest first)
1. ________________	1. ________________	1. ________________
2. ________________	2. ________________	2. ________________
3. ________________	3. ________________	3. ________________
4. ________________	4. ________________	4. ________________
5. ________________	5. ________________	5. ________________

ALL MIXED UP

Some lists of words start with different letters. Other lists start with the same letter. When two words begin with the same letter, alphabetize by the second letter. If the second letters are the same, alphabetize by the third letter.

Example: Jack
Joe
John

A. *Directions:* Arrange the words in each list in alphabetical order. Work as fast as you can. Do one list at a time.

List 1:		**List 2:**		**List 3:**	
new	______________	lift	______________	Beth	______________
now	______________	letter	______________	Barbie	______________
none	______________	less	______________	Bunny	______________
nice	______________	long	______________	Bob	______________
nine	______________	length	______________	Bill	______________

When two words have the same beginning letters, the shorter word comes first. A word without an apostrophe comes before one with an apostrophe.

Examples: are
aren't

B. *Directions:* Use all the rules you have learned.
Put each of these lists in alphabetical order.

List 1:		**List 2:**		**List 3:**	
is	______________	meat	______________	June	______________
its	______________	me	______________	Jim	______________
it's	______________	mean	______________	Jimmy	______________
isn't	______________	meant	______________	Jane	______________
it	______________	meet	______________	Jan	______________

SORTING PRACTICE

To get very good at sorting, we need lots of practice.

A. ***Directions:*** Sort this list of food into three lists according to the meal it will be served.

Sliced peaches	Fried chicken	Cream of broccoli soup
Scrambled eggs and bacon	Sweet potatoes	Jello with whipped cream
Tossed salad	Two cookies	Brussels sprouts
Milk	Rolls and butter	Toast and jelly
Orange juice	Tuna sandwich	Hot tea with lemon

Breakfast	**Lunch**	**Dinner**
____________	____________	____________
____________	____________	____________
____________	____________	____________
____________	____________	____________
____________	____________	____________
____________	____________	____________
____________	____________	____________
____________	____________	____________

B. ***Directions:*** Sort the following vegetables. Write the list in order from your most favorite to your least favorite.

corn	tomatoes	squash	broccoli	asparagus
peas	green beans	potatoes	cabbage	lima beans
beets	peppers	turnips	radishes	lettuce

1. ____________
2. ____________
3. ____________
4. ____________
5. ____________
6. ____________
7. ____________
8. ____________
9. ____________
10. ____________
11. ____________
12. ____________
13. ____________
14. ____________
15. ____________

NUMERICAL ORDER

Many times we list things in order according to their numerical value.

A. ***Directions:*** Write the list of clothing below according to their cost. List the clothes from least expensive to most expensive.

Sweater	$25	Shoes	$45	Cap	$5
Tee Shirt	$12	Socks	$3	Jacket	$43
Slacks	$32	Shorts	$15	Bathrobe	$24

1. ____________________
2. ____________________
3. ____________________
4. ____________________
5. ____________________
6. ____________________
7. ____________________
8. ____________________
9. ____________________

B. ***Directions:*** Below is a list of breads and cereals and the number of calories per serving. Sort the list in two ways.

Breads and Cereals	
Roll, 100	Melba toast, 20
Cornmeal muffin, 140	Rye bread, 75
French toast, 105	White bread, 60
Doughnut, 120	Pretzel, 7

List the foods from the most calories to the fewest.

1. ____________________
2. ____________________
3. ____________________
4. ____________________
5. ____________________
6. ____________________
7. ____________________
8. ____________________

List by calories, fewest to most.

1. ____________________
2. ____________________
3. ____________________
4. ____________________
5. ____________________
6. ____________________
7. ____________________
8. ____________________

UNIT 6 REVIEW: Proofread, Revise, Recopy

Sorting is important in many different everyday situations. See how quickly and accurately you can sort these lists.

A. *Directions:* Sort this list of meats according to calories. Start with the one that has the fewest calories per serving.

liver, 85	chicken, 200	turkey, 315
sausage, 95	veal cutlet, 285	frankfurter, 100
chipped beef, 115	hamburger, 150	pork, 330

1. ________________ 4. ________________ 7. ________________
2. ________________ 5. ________________ 8. ________________
3. ________________ 6. ________________ 9. ________________

Karen's favorite books are:

Rebecca of Sunnybrook Farm by Kate Douglas Wiggin
Jane Eyre by Charlotte Bronte
Wuthering Heights by Emily Bronte
Lad, A Dog by Alfred Payson Terhune
Lassie Come Home by Eric Knight
Black Beauty by Anna Sewell
Tom Sawyer by Mark Twain
Pride and Prejudice by Jane Austen

B. *Directions:* Write Karen's list of books in alphabetical order by title.

1. ________________________ 5. ________________________
2. ________________________ 6. ________________________
3. ________________________ 7. ________________________
4. ________________________ 8. ________________________

▶ Now list them in order by the last name of the author. This is the way you'd find them on a library shelf.

1. ________________________ 5. ________________________
2. ________________________ 6. ________________________
3. ________________________ 7. ________________________
4. ________________________ 8. ________________________

Unit 7
Directions

GETTING FROM HERE TO THERE

When you write directions, you should describe each turn.

Examples: Turn right on 4th street.
or
Go down Main Street for 2 blocks. Then, turn right on 5th Street.

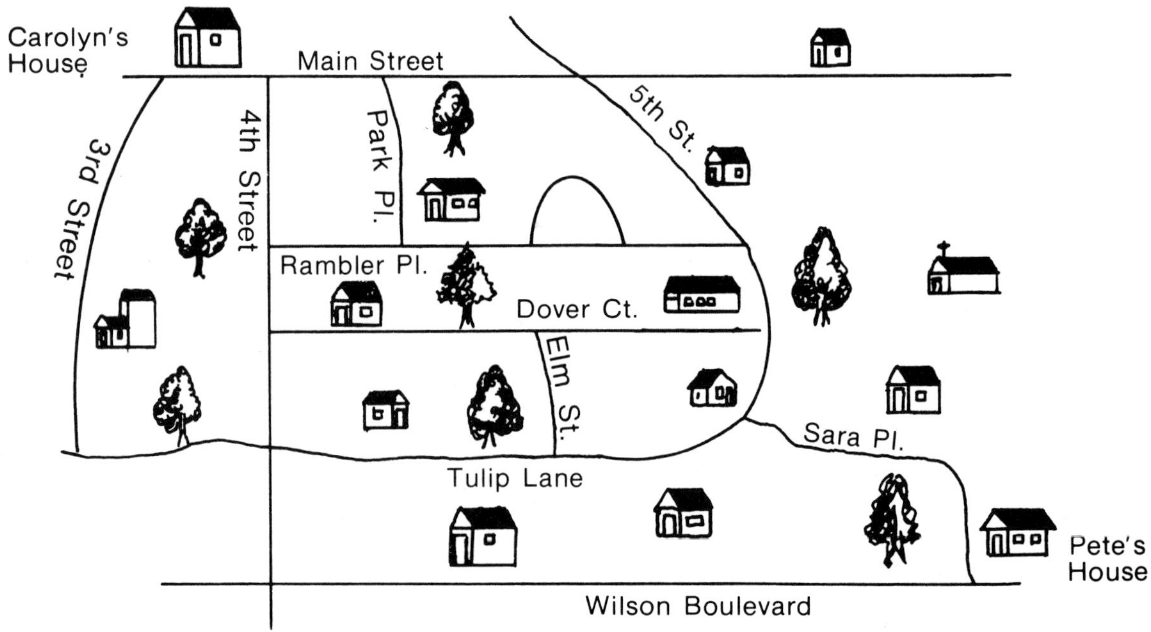

Directions: Use the map to write the directions to get from Carolyn's house to Pete's house. Describe every turn.

____

____

____

____

____

____

WRITING DIRECTIONS

In our everyday life, we often give people directions to our homes.

Here are the directions to Roger's house. Study them carefully.

1. Get on the Beltway going south.
2. Go east on Exit 17, George Washington Highway.
3. Drive about 12 miles and then turn north on Cooperstown Road.
4. Go three miles, through two lights, past the Cooperstown High School.
5. Turn right at the third light at the gas station.
6. Go two blocks and turn left on Carter Drive.
7. Drive one and a half blocks.
8. Look for a blue and white Rambler on your right.

Directions: Write directions to your house. Start with where you are right now. Describe each turn.

____

____

____

____

____

____

____

____

____

► Exchange your paper with a friend. Ask if the directions are clear.

MAPMAKING

People often make up a map to show others how to get to their homes.

Here's an example:

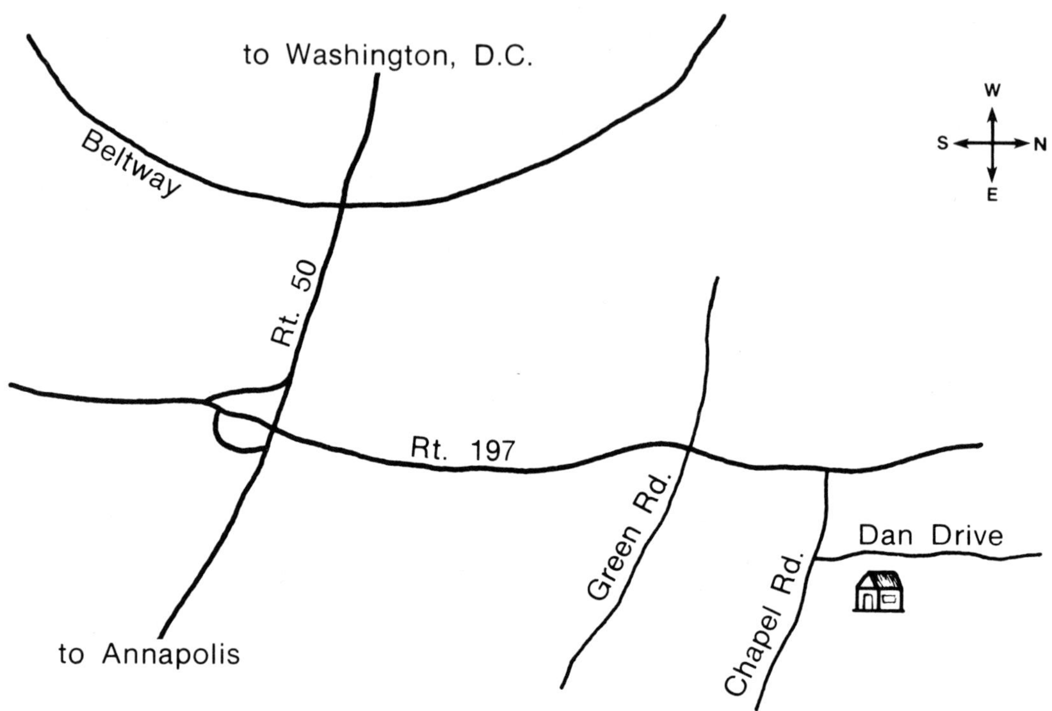

Directions: Use the space below to draw a map to your house from where you are right now.

RECORDING DIRECTIONS

Recording directions requires you to be a careful listener.

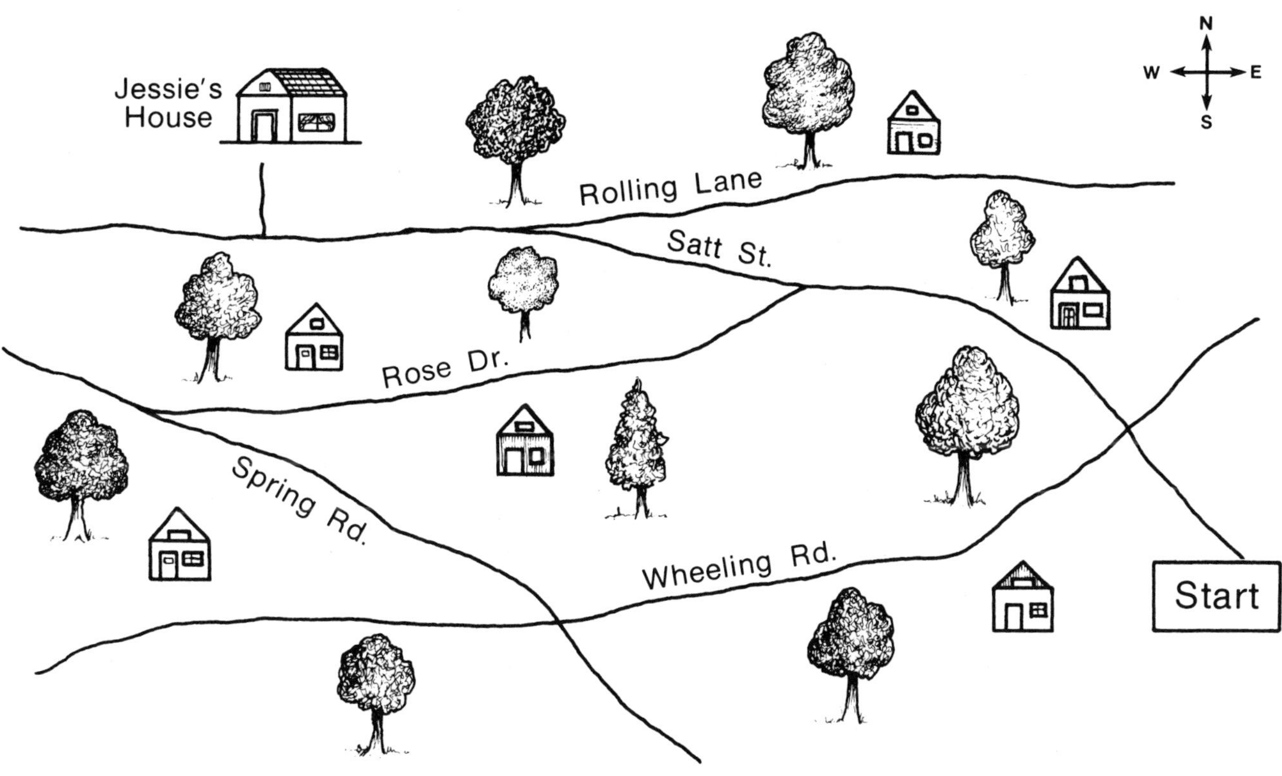

Directions: Ask someone to use the map to give you directions to Jessie's house. You are to write the directions as they are given to you. Write the directions in the space below.

____

____

____

____

____

____

____

Compare your directions with the map.

UNIT 7 REVIEW: Proofread, Revise, Recopy

Poor directions will get you or your friends lost.

Directions: Study the map carefully. Read the directions to go from Emma's house to Anna's house. Find the mistakes. Edit and revise the directions to make them better. Write the revised directions on the lines below.

1. Drive southeast on Nelson Street. Cross Roger's Rd.
2. Turn on Rt. 70 and watch for the court.
3. Go right. Then turn on Rose Lane. Look for my house.

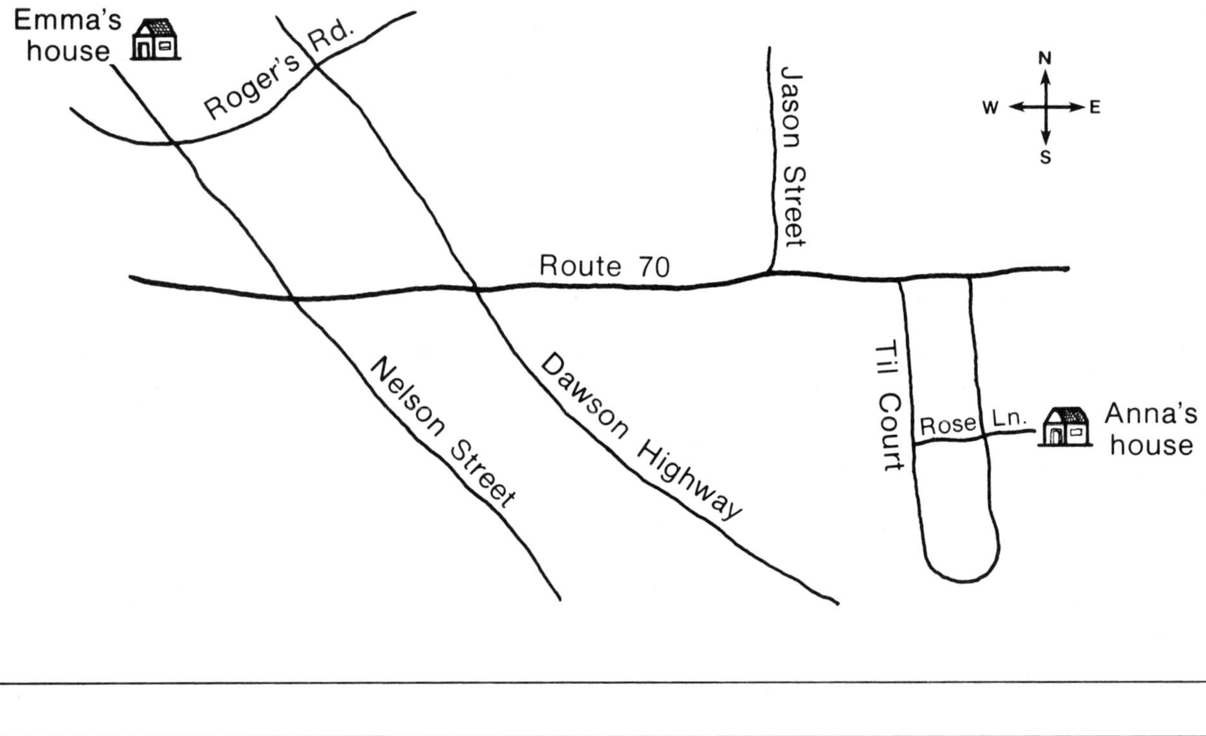

Unit 8
Sentence Rules

RECOGNIZING SENTENCES

There are just a few rules that you need to know about sentences.

Rule 1: Every sentence expresses a complete thought.

A. *Directions:* Write *Yes* on the line beside the group of words that is a sentence. Write *No* if the group of words is not a sentence. Be prepared to explain your answer.

_________ 1. Gone with the wind.
_________ 2. My typewriter is broken.
_________ 3. Her new sweatshirt is purple.
_________ 4. Lucky number three.
_________ 5. My favorite quotation.
_________ 6. The workers enjoyed using the computer.

Rule 2: Capitalize the first word in every sentence.

B. *Directions:* Capitalize the first word in each sentence. Cross out the lower-case letter. Write the correction above it.

in the eighteenth century, James Watt was working on the steam engine. that invention revolutionized travel. in the twentieth century, engineers and scientists are working on space travel. do you think you will ever travel in space? that certainly would be exciting.

BEGINNING A SENTENCE

A. *Directions:* Rewrite these sentences. Capitalize the first word of each sentence.

1. start your sentence with a capital letter, please.

 ____

2. an Apple is a type of computer.

 ____

3. wipe the mud off your shoes, Sammy. thanks.

 ____

4. did anyone see the pencil with my name on it?

 ____

5. the postal carrier usually comes about one o'clock.

 ____

Rule 3:	Every sentence ends with a mark of punctuation. Never end a sentence with a comma.

B. *Directions:* Find the end of each sentence. Put the correct mark of punctuation. Do not use commas to end sentences.

In the morning at five o'clock, the alarm clock rings
It is really too early for anyone to wake up Don't you agree
I have a clock radio I listen to music for a while Finally, I
have to get up Wow What a drag

ENDING A SENTENCE

Every sentence ends with a mark of punctuation. Punctuation marks are like road signs. A period, an exclamation mark, or a question mark all say STOP. A comma says SLOW DOWN or PAUSE. A sentence's end mark depends on what type of sentence it is.

• Statements end with a period.	My name is Sheila.
• Commands or requests end with periods, too.	Please pass the butter.
• Questions end with question marks.	What's your name again?
• Exclamatory sentences end with exclamation marks.	I said my name is Sheila!

Directions: Identify each sentence as a *statement*, a *command* or *request*, a *question*, or an *exclamatory* sentence. Write your answer on the line before the sentence. Add the correct mark of punctuation at the end of each sentence.

____________________ 1. That noise is driving me crazy

____________________ 2. Please stop that noise

____________________ 3. This music is not noise

____________________ 4. It sounds like noise to me

____________________ 5. Why won't you give this music a chance

____________________ 6. Give my music a chance first

____________________ 7. No, No, I can't stand opera

____________________ 8. Can we make a bargain

____________________ 9. I'll listen to yours, and you listen to mine

____________________ 10. Turnabout is fair play, I always say

FOR YOU TO DO:

1. Write two examples of each kind of sentence on your own paper.
2. Try to make your sentences tell a story.

COMPOUND SENTENCES

A compound sentence is really two related sentences joined together with a conjunction.

These are examples of conjunctions that connect two sentences: *and, but, or, nor,* and *for.* You cannot connect two sentences with just a comma.

Wrong: Bully is a Labrador retriever, Coco is a toy poodle.
Right: Bully is a Labrador retriver, **and** Coco is a toy poodle.
Right: Bully is a Labrador retriever. Coco is a toy poodle.

A. *Directions:* Read each group of words carefully. Write *Right* on the line before the sentence if it is correctly written as a sentence. Write *Wrong* on the line if it is not written correctly. Rewrite the sentences correctly.

__________ 1. Jerry and Sue like tennis they play as often as they can.

____

__________ 2. Write in complete sentences, your grades will improve.

____

__________ 3. Many afternoons we met at the ball field, and we played until dark.

____

__________ 4. Last night Tom read his book several hours today he is sleepy.

____

B. *Directions:* Rewrite each sentence below so that it is a compound sentence. Remember to add a conjunction. Underline the conjunction.

1. Jay plays basketball. He hopes his team will win the championship.

____

____

2. Bill and Ralph met at the gym. They both lifted weights.

____

____

UNIT 8 REVIEW: Proofread, Revise, Recopy

Always check the sentences that you write.

Directions: Read the story below. Find the mistakes. Rewrite the story correctly.

in the spring Chris decided to play soccer her new team practiced every Tuesday and Thursday afternoons they met at Spring Lake Sports Park. Have you ever heard of it. This park was built by the city government for the people to use her coaches decided Chris would be a good goalie, she was happy because that was her favorite position

Unit 9
Messages and Memos

IS IT COMPLETE?

In our everyday life we often write messages.

A *message* is an informal written communication. We often call it a *note*. A *memo* (or memorandum) is a formal message.

Kinds of information you may include in a message:

- The name of the person the message is for.
- The name of the person the message is from.
- The time and date you wrote the message.
- Any facts you want the person to know.

Directions: Read each message. Then write what is missing.

Example: Mom. I'll be home later. Ted

The time and date of the message are missing.

1. Ted. Sorry I missed you. Mom

 ____

2. Ann. Martin called. Call him back. Love, Sara

 ____

3. Mr. Smith. I stopped by to find out about my homework assignment, but you were out. I'll come back later.

 ____

4. Dad. Someone called about your meeting. Love, Mickey

 ____

MESSAGES AT HOME

Directions: Read the conversation below.
Then write the message in the space below.

Christy: I am going to be late.

Janet: Where are you?

Christy: I'm still at school at band practice. We have to rehearse for at least another hour.

Janet: When will you be home?

Christy: Rehearsal is over at 5 P.M., but I need a ride home. Have Mom pick me up.

Janet: She's not home yet and I'm going out.

Christy: Please leave her a message.

Janet: OK. See you at dinner.

Write the message here:

Message

Directions: Write a message to your friend. Tell him about tonight's homework. Include the time and date. Be sure to have your name and your friend's name. WRITE NEATLY!

RECORDING HOMEWORK ASSIGNMENTS

Sometimes you need to write messages to yourself. Take just as much time and be just as careful as you would if the note were for someone else.

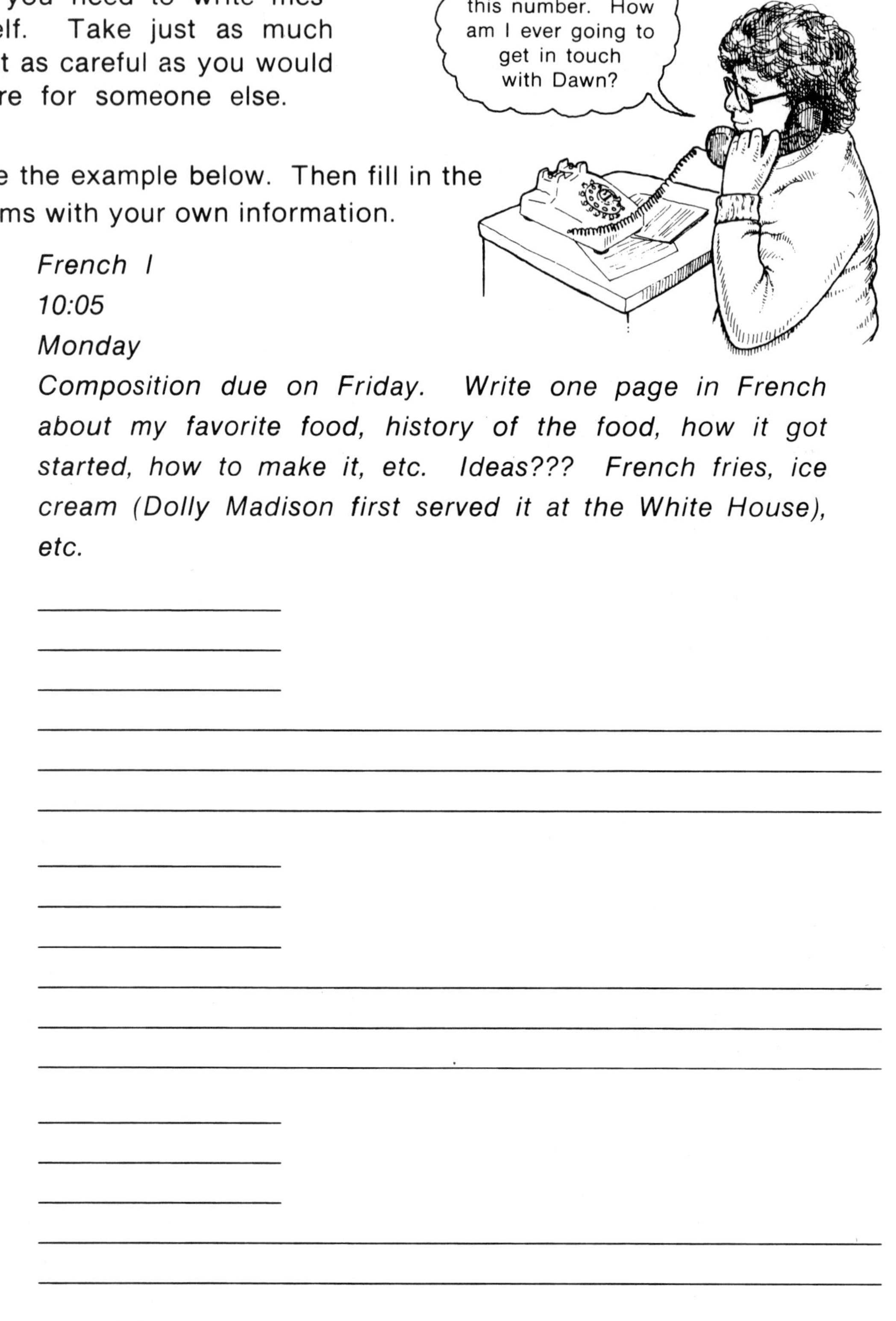

Directions: Use the example below. Then fill in the forms with your own information.

SUBJECT: *French I*
TIME: *10:05*
DATE: *Monday*
ASSIGNMENT: *Composition due on Friday. Write one page in French about my favorite food, history of the food, how it got started, how to make it, etc. Ideas??? French fries, ice cream (Dolly Madison first served it at the White House), etc.*

SUBJECT: ________________
TIME: ________________
DATE: ________________
ASSIGNMENT: ____
____
____

SUBJECT: ________________
TIME: ________________
DATE: ________________
ASSIGNMENT: ____
____
____

SUBJECT: ________________
TIME: ________________
DATE: ________________
ASSIGNMENT: ____
____
____

MESSAGES AT WORK

At a job, you will often take messages for other people. Many times the company will have a formal message pad.

Directions:

Use the information below to fill in the message forms.

Mr. Jones.
Janet called at 3 P.M., March 3, and wants you to call her back at 555-3423.

To__________
Date__________ Time__________

WHILE YOU WERE OUT

M__________
of__________
Phone__________
Area Code Number Extension

TELEPHONED		PLEASE CALL	
CALLED TO SEE YOU		WILL CALL AGAIN	
WANTS TO SEE YOU		URGENT	
	RETURNED YOUR CALL		

Message__________

Operator

Mr. Lee:
Mrs. Johnson stopped by to see you. She wants to order a dozen roses. Send them to her house, Friday, March 12.

To__________
Date__________ Time__________

WHILE YOU WERE OUT

M__________
of__________
Phone__________
Area Code Number Extension

TELEPHONED		PLEASE CALL	
CALLED TO SEE YOU		WILL CALL AGAIN	
WANTS TO SEE YOU		URGENT	
	RETURNED YOUR CALL		

Message__________

Operator

ADS AND ANNOUNCEMENTS

The word **ad** is an abbreviation for *advertisement.* We are familiar with commercials on television and the radio. We have all seen ads in magazines.

> When you want to sell something, you can put an ad in the newspaper.

An **announcement** is a public message. We use announcements to advertise events.

> - You might prepare an announcement for the public address system.
> - You might design a flyer, make copies, and distribute it.
> - You might make a poster.

Some guidelines for all advertising are as follows:

> - Make your message short and to the point.
> - Include all the necessary details.
> - Include some attention-getting words.
> - Be sure it is accurate in every way.

Directions: Write an advertisement for the school newspaper to sell a used book or some other object. Keep it under 25 words.

____

____

____

____

____

Directions: Write an announcement for the public address system. Tell everyone that try-outs will be held for a school play. Include the date, time, and place. Make everyone want to come.

____

____

____

____

____

WRITING ADS

What do you have for sale? You may be able to sell it by putting an advertisement in your local newspaper.

Directions: Study the sample ads.

Automobiles, Domestic

JEEP — '49, CJ3 ex-military jeep, 230 V-6 Buick eng. Excel. shape. $1600. Call 555-1245.

LINCOLN — Town car, 4DR, white on white w/red leather interior. Special value $18,000. Visit Rodney's Lincoln Center, 1900 South Boulevard.

Write your own ad to sell a car. Write in the box. You may use some of the suggested words below.

Suggestions: Orig. owner (original owner). New tires. Good condition. MUST SELL! Fully loaded. Only driven on Sundays. Like new. Very clean. Great buy! Well maintained. Best offer. Fully equipped. Specially priced.

Directions: Write an advertisement for a garage sale. Sell things that you own that you no longer need or want.

Write the ad here. Keep it to 50 words or less.

Unit 10
Letter Writing

KINDS OF LETTERS

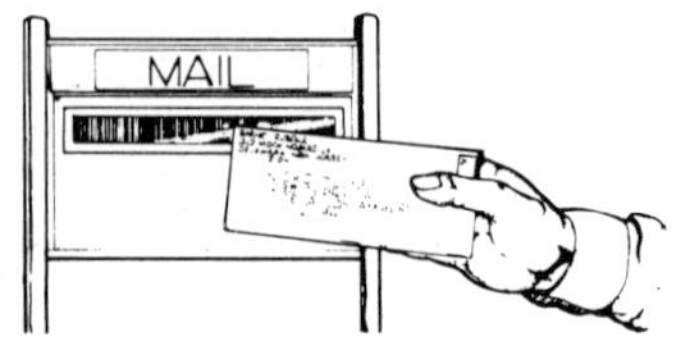

We leave a message or a memo, but we usually put letters in the mail.

There are two kinds of letters: personal and business.

Personal Letter
The form is very simple.

May 3

Dear Alice,

We are looking forward to your visit with us next week. It's been such a long time since we visited last. I hope you plan to stay for at least a week.

Please let us know exactly what time to pick you up at the bus stop.

Love,

Florence

Business Letter
This letter has more parts.

12 Harrison Drive
Smalltown, USA 87653
May 3, 19__

Mrs. Carla Tower
Johnson Press
One Silver Circle
Washington, D.C. 22002

Dear Mrs. Tower:

I am enclosing a short story for your consideration. It is about a young boy on his first camping trip. Enclosed is a self-addressed stamped envelope for its return.

Sincerely yours,
Howard D'Mara
Howard D'Mara

Directions: Can you identify the parts of a letter? Match Column A with Column B.

1. Sincerely yours,	____ A. Addressee
2. Dear Alice,	____ B. Body
3. I am enclosing a....	____ C. Salutation
4. 12 Harrison Drive Smalltown, USA 87653	____ D. Closing
5. Mrs. Carla Tower	____ E. Return address

A THANK-YOU NOTE

People today use the telephone to talk to their friends more often than they write letters. However, a thank-you note is always expected in certain situations. Always write a note to thank people for a gift or when you have been a guest in someone's home.

Directions:
Study the sample letter.

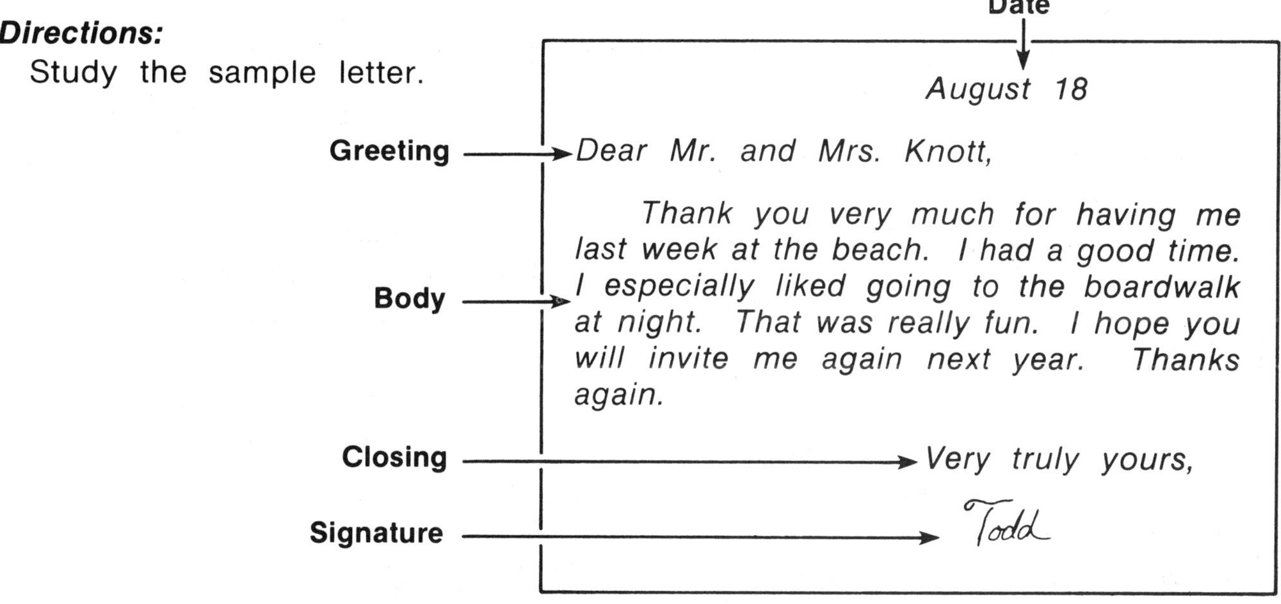
Date

August 18

Greeting → *Dear Mr. and Mrs. Knott,*

Body → *Thank you very much for having me last week at the beach. I had a good time. I especially liked going to the boardwalk at night. That was really fun. I hope you will invite me again next year. Thanks again.*

Closing → *Very truly yours,*

Signature → *Todd*

Directions: Write a thank-you letter to someone you know.
Suggestions: Thank someone who gave you a present on your last birthday.
Thank someone who invited you to their house for a party.
Thank someone who did something nice for you.

INVITATIONS

If you want to invite people to an event, you can buy packages of invitations at the store, or you can write your own.

Include information like this:

- The event (party, weekend, dinner)
- The time and date
- The place
- The cost (if any)
- What the person should bring or wear

> Dear Club Members:
>
> You are invited to an Open House on Monday, March 10 at 7:30 P.M. Come to the Laurel Woods Community Center. Punch and cookies will be served. Dress casually.
>
> Sincerely,
> The Open House Committee

Directions: Read the invitation below. Proofread for mistakes. Make corrections. Add missing information. Recopy the invitation with the changes.

> *Dear Fred, I'm having a party and I'd like you to come. Bring potato chips and sodas. Let me know if you can come. Joe*

Write your invitation here. Use your imagination to add the information Joe left out.

ADDRESSING AN ENVELOPE

If you do not address the envelope correctly, your letter may never arrive. Be sure to put on the right amount of postage.

Addressing an envelope is very simple.

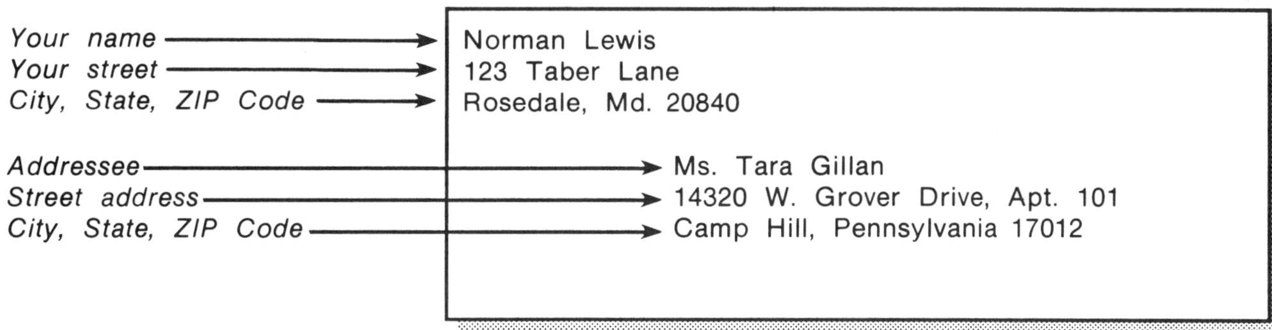

Directions: Here are some sample addresses. They are all wrong in some way. Rewrite them correctly.

1. Brown, Valerie ____________________
   1231 Santa Anna Parkway ____________________
   San Jose, 95129 ____________________
   CA ____________________

2. Bob Aleshire, Apt. 3A ____________________
   Grifton, NC 28530 ____________________
   Johnson Drive 1231 ____________________

3. Johnny Kochert ____________________
   6034 Heatherwood Drive, VA ____________________
   Alexandria, 22150 ____________________

4. Joanie Matthews ____________________
   21234 Dawson Street ____________________
   Alaska, Apt. 2 ____________________
   Juneau 99801 ____________________

5. Roy Theuret ____________________
   16510 ____________________
   12 Howard Place ____________________
   Erie PA ____________________

PARTS OF A BUSINESS LETTER

General Rules for Business Letters:
- Use stationery $8\frac{1}{2}$ by 11 inches.
- Business letters should be typed.
- Use only one side of the paper.

The greeting, or salutation, in a business letter includes the title and last name of the addressee.

Dear Dr. Vereb: Dear Mr. Smith: Dear Rev. Leonard:

Choose your favorite complimentary close. Here are some examples:

Sincerely,	Sincerely yours,	Very truly yours,
Cordially,	Yours truly,	Respectfully yours,

Directions: Label each part of this business letter. Use the words below.

Vantage Systems
1900 West Collington Road
Suite 100
Washington, D.C. 20002 — A. ____________

January 12, 19__ — B. ____________

Ms. Ann Garman
4023 Wharton Drive
Collegeville, PA 19426 — C. ____________

Dear Ms. Garman: — D. ____________

Vantage Systems is pleased to offer you the position of office manager starting January 23. Your company benefits are explained in the policy brochure which I have attached. We are looking forward to having you join us. — E. ____________

Sincerely yours, — F. ____________

Linda Owens — G. ____________

Linda Owens
Personnel Manager — H. ____________

Enclosure

Date	Typed Name and Title	Inside Address	Salutation
Body	Complimentary Close	Signature	Heading

A LETTER OF APPLICATION

One of the most common types of business letters is a letter of application. You write these letters when you apply for a job.

Directions:
- Study the sample help-wanted ad from a newspaper.
- Write a letter asking for the job.
- Use your own name and address for the return address.

OFFICE HELPER WANTED. We are looking for someone willing to work in a small office. Duties include filing, running errands, and other jobs for our busy staff. Write a letter of application to Best Office Supplies, c/o Lacy Marks, 9000 Van Buren Blvd., Suite 12, Reading, MA 01867

SPECIAL KINDS OF LETTERS

- **Letter to the Editor**
  One of the ways you can express your opinions is by writing a letter to the editor of a newspaper. The editor will often print your letter if you write it neatly and express .your ideas clearly.

- **Letter of Complaint**
  People often order items through the mail. If you return an item that you don't like, you will need to write down what is wrong with the product.

Dear Sir:

In my opinion, the city should definitely build a new ball park. The current one does not have enough seating capacity to attract a major ball team. We have been without a team for many years now.

Yours truly,
Julie Larson
Julie Larson

Dear Sir:

I am returning the sweater I ordered. It does not look at all like the one pictured in the catalog. I would like you to refund my money.

Sincerely yours,
Oliver Allyn
Oliver Allyn

Directions: Write either a letter to the editor or a letter of complaint. Supply the name and address of the addressee.

UNIT 10 REVIEW: Proofread, Revise, Recopy

Directions: Proofread, Revise, and Recopy the business letter below. Be sure the greeting and closing are appropriate for a business letter. Check the spelling and sentence structure. Use a dictionary if necessary. Be sure the letter has all its parts!

Mr. Fred Jackson
Flint, Michigan 48504
2121 Howard Road
April 3, 19__

1213 Superior Lane
George Wilson & Sons, Reality Company
Flint, Michigan 48504

Hi! Mr. Wilson:

As we discussed on the telephone, i'd like you to seel our house. We hope to move from the area within the next two months, the price of the house will include the rugs, all appliances and the drapes and curtains, and we are having the house painted as you suggested and that should be finished this week.

See you all later,
Fred

Unit 11
Completing Forms

FILLING OUT AN ORDER FORM

In our everyday lives we all fill out different kinds of forms. Here are three basic rules:

1. Fill in every space. Answer every question.
2. Be sure the information is accurate.
3. Write neatly. Print with a pen, or type.

A. ***Directions:*** Fill in the following form for ordering address labels.

Complete this form and mail to: Thomasina Rivera, Inc.
Box 5555 Grand Central Station
New York, NY 10001

How Many?	Name and Address, 3 lines	Price	Total
		$2.50 per hundred	

B. ***Directions:*** Answer these questions about the form above.

1. Did you write your full name? ____________
2. What is your house number? ________________
3. What is your street name? ____
4. If you live in an apartment, what is the number? ____________
5. Did you include the name of your city, state, and ZIP Code? ____________
6. What is the name of your city? ______________________________
7. What is the name of your state? ______________________________
8. What is your ZIP Code? ________________
9. What is the abbreviation for your state? ________________

THE JOB APPLICATION

One of the most important forms you will ever fill out is the job application form. The way you fill out a form will determine whether you will get a job interview.

1. Fill in every space. Answer every question.
2. Be sure the information is accurate.
3. Write neatly. Print with a pen, or type.

Usually there are four types of questions to answer:

1. Personal Information — questions about you!
2. Work Experience — jobs you have had.
3. Educational Background — your schooling.
4. References — people who know about you, your work, your credit.

If a question does not apply to you, write *N/A*, the abbreviation for *not applicable*, in the space.

PERSONAL INFORMATION: Please type or print.

Name Jordan, Nancy H. Phone (912) 883-5555
Last First Middle (area code) (number)

Address 17 Vantage Lane Albany, GA 31707
Number Street City State ZIP Code

Social Security Number 571-36-2605 Are you a US Citizen? (Yes) No

Date of birth 5-10-60 Place of birth Belleville, IL

Marital status ✓ single ___ married ___ divorced ___ widowed

Number of dependents 0 Military status N/A

Directions: Complete the practice application form. Use information about yourself.

PERSONAL INFORMATION: Please type or print.

Name ______________________ Phone ______________
Last First Middle (area code) (number)

Address ____
Number Street City State ZIP Code

Social Security Number ______________ Are you a US Citizen? Yes No

Date of birth ______________ Place of birth ______________

Marital status ___ single ___ married ___ divorced ___ widowed

Number of dependents ______________ Military status ______________

JOB APPLICATION: Educational Background

Your educational background includes all of the schools you have attended. Your employer may wish to obtain your transcripts. A *transcript* is an official list of the courses you have taken and the grades you received.

	Elementary	High	College/ University	Graduate/ Professional
School Name and Location	Central School Springdale, PA	Albany High School Albany, GA	Melville Jr. College Melville, GA	
Years Completed: (Circle)	4 5 (6) 7 8	9 10 11 (12)	1 (2) 3 4	1 2 3 4
Diploma/ Degree		June, 1980	A.A. June, 1982	
Describe Course Of Study:		Academic	Communications	
Describe specialized training:	Art classes, Albany Art Center, 5 years			
List other skills:	Drawing, lettering			

Directions: Complete the practice application form. Write about your education.

	Elementary	High	College/ University	Graduate/ Professional
School Name and Location				
Years Completed: (Circle)	4 5 6 7 8	9 10 11 12	1 2 3 4	1 2 3 4
Diploma/ Degree				
Describe Course Of Study:				
Describe specialized training:				
List other skills:				

JOB APPLICATION: Work Experience

Your work experience includes all the jobs you have ever had. You can also list volunteer work experience for which you were not paid. Keep a record of your employment history in case you ever decide to change jobs.

Employment History

List each job held. Start with your present or last job. Include military service assignments and volunteer activities.

<table>
<tr><td rowspan="2">1</td><td rowspan="2">Employer: George's Decorating</td><td colspan="2">Dates</td><td rowspan="2">Work Performed</td></tr>
<tr><td>From</td><td>To</td></tr>
<tr><td></td><td>Address: 226 Jefferson Pl., Albany, GA</td><td>8/83</td><td>Present</td><td>Interior Coordination</td></tr>
<tr><td></td><td rowspan="2">Job Title: Decorator</td><td colspan="2">Hrly. Rate/Salary</td><td rowspan="2">and space</td></tr>
<tr><td>Starting</td><td>Final</td></tr>
<tr><td></td><td>Supervisor: Louise Brown</td><td rowspan="2">$6.50</td><td rowspan="2">$7.00 plus comm.</td><td>planning.</td></tr>
<tr><td></td><td>Reason for Leaving: N/A</td><td></td></tr>
<tr><td rowspan="2">2</td><td rowspan="2">Employer: Roland's Art Center</td><td colspan="2">Dates</td><td rowspan="2">Work Performed</td></tr>
<tr><td>From</td><td>To</td></tr>
<tr><td></td><td>Address: 902 Hamilton Ave., Albany, GA</td><td>8/82</td><td>7/83</td><td>Ordering material,</td></tr>
<tr><td></td><td rowspan="2">Job Title: Assistant Manager</td><td colspan="2">Hrly. Rate/Salary</td><td rowspan="2">scheduling employees,</td></tr>
<tr><td>Starting</td><td>Final</td></tr>
<tr><td></td><td>Supervisor: Roland West</td><td rowspan="2">$4.50</td><td rowspan="2">$5.50</td><td>customer service.</td></tr>
<tr><td></td><td>Reason for Leaving: To accept better position</td><td></td></tr>
</table>

Directions: Complete the practice application form. Write about your work experience.

<table>
<tr><td rowspan="2">1</td><td rowspan="2">Employer:</td><td colspan="2">Dates</td><td rowspan="2">Work Performed</td></tr>
<tr><td>From</td><td>To</td></tr>
<tr><td></td><td>Address:</td><td></td><td></td><td></td></tr>
<tr><td></td><td rowspan="2">Job Title:</td><td colspan="2">Hrly. Rate/Salary</td><td rowspan="2"></td></tr>
<tr><td>Starting</td><td>Final</td></tr>
<tr><td></td><td>Supervisor:</td><td rowspan="2"></td><td rowspan="2"></td><td></td></tr>
<tr><td></td><td>Reason for Leaving:</td><td></td></tr>
<tr><td rowspan="2">2</td><td rowspan="2">Employer:</td><td colspan="2">Dates</td><td rowspan="2">Work Performed</td></tr>
<tr><td>From</td><td>To</td></tr>
<tr><td></td><td>Address:</td><td></td><td></td><td></td></tr>
<tr><td></td><td rowspan="2">Job Title:</td><td colspan="2">Hrly. Rate/Salary</td><td rowspan="2"></td></tr>
<tr><td>Starting</td><td>Final</td></tr>
<tr><td></td><td>Supervisor:</td><td rowspan="2"></td><td rowspan="2"></td><td></td></tr>
<tr><td></td><td>Reason for Leaving:</td><td></td></tr>
</table>

JOB APPLICATION: References

A reference is a recommendation from a person who knows you. Be sure to present only people who will give you a "good" report. Always call these people to ask if you may use their names as references.

There are three kinds of references:
- Work references — people who know about your job skills.
- Credit references — people who know about your bill paying history.
- Personal references — people who know about your character.

Work references are former and current employers or teachers.
Credit references are people who have loaned you money, such as a bank or a store.
Personal references can be clergy, neighbors, teachers, and other people who have known you for a long time. Do not ask a relative to be a reference.

REFERENCES

Name	Address	Phone	Position
1. George Kurtz	226 Jefferson Place	860-2511	Owner, George's
	Albany, Georgia 31702		Decorating
2. Roland West	902 Hamilton Ave.	883-2000	President,
	Albany, Georgia 31711		Roland's Art Center

A. *Directions:* Complete the practice application form.
Give information about people who know you.

Name	Address	Phone	Position

B. *Directions:* Fill in each blank with one of the words below.

1. Joe asked his ______________ for a job ______________.
2. When will you be ______________ to begin your new __________?
3. What is your current ______________?
4. Since Mary was not married, her marital status is ______________.
5. Tom's wife and baby son were his ______________.

supervisor	reference	available	position	salary
dependents	single	military	transcript	

ABBREVIATIONS ON FORMS

Read the instructions on a form very carefully. Be especially careful about abbreviations. Most forms use abbreviations to save space.

Common Abbreviations

No. or # .... Number	P.O. Box .... Post Office Box
Tel. No. .... Telephone Number	POB .... Post Office Box
Ext. or X .. Telephone Extension Number	ACCT. .... Account
D.O.B. .... Date of Birth	MO. .... Month
M.I. .... Middle Initial	YR. .... Year
SOC. SEC. # .... Social Security Number	APT. .... Apartment

A. *Directions:* Complete the following form.
Use the list of abbreviations to help you.

Bank Card Application Form

NAME ______________________________
Last First M.I.

ADDRESS ______________________________
No. Street Apt. #

____
City State ZIP

SOC. SEC. NO. _____-_____-________ D.O.B. ___/___/___

TEL. NO. ______________________ EXT. __________

OTHER ACCT. WITH THIS BANK? ( ) Yes ( ) No

If yes, #____________________

Do you wish to apply for a Bank Chg. Acct? ( ) Yes ( ) No

B. *Directions:* Rewrite each of the following phrases. Write out any abbreviations.

1. Bank Acct. No. ______________________
2. POB 34 ______________________
3. SOC. SEC. # ______________________
4. Apt. 101 ______________________
5. 249-1330 Ext. 34 ______________________

WRITING CHECKS

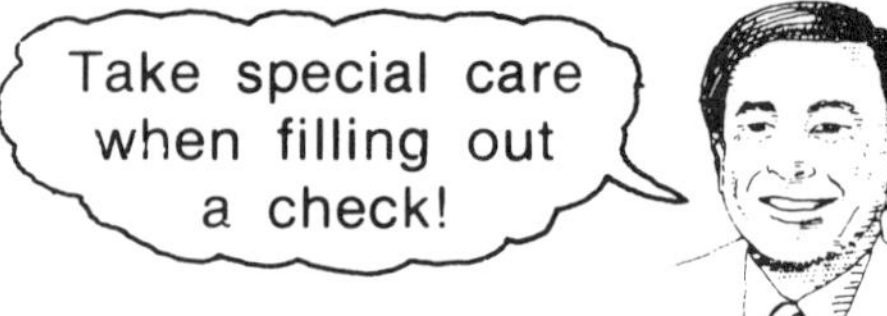

Study the sample check below. Every blank has been filled in.

Charlotte A. Marmo
4590 Tulip Drive
Elizabethtown, PA 17022
(717) 367-5555

786

May 3 19 89

78-463
340

PAY TO THE ORDER OF Suburban Furniture $ 125.35

One hundred twenty-five and 35/100 DOLLARS

First National Bank

FOR lamps

Charlotte A. Marmo

⑈003332⑈ ⑆052000618⑆ 6265936⑈

A. ***Directions:*** Answer these questions about the sample check above.

1. What is the check number? ______
2. On what date did Charlotte Marmo write this check? ______
3. Who can cash this check? ______
4. What is the amount of this check? ______
5. What is this check for? ______
6. Who wrote this check? ______

B. ***Directions:*** Complete the check below.
Pay a bill to the "Electric Company" for $47.04.

Charlotte A. Marmo
4590 Tulip Drive
Elizabethtown, PA 17022
(717) 367-5555

787

______ 19____

78-463
340

PAY TO THE ORDER OF ______ $ ______

______ DOLLARS

First National Bank

FOR ______ ______

⑈003332⑈ ⑆052000618⑆ 6265936⑈

NUMBER WORDS ON CHECKS

On a check you write the amount twice. First you write the amount in numbers. Then you write the amount in words.

Number Words				
	one	ten	nineteen	eighty
	two	eleven	twenty	ninety
	three	twelve	twenty-one	one hundred
	four	thirteen	thirty	one hundred one
	five	fourteen	thirty-one	two hundred
	six	fifteen	forty	one thousand
	seven	sixteen	fifty	one thousand, one hundred, one
	eight	seventeen	sixty	
	nine	eighteen	seventy	

A. ***Directions:*** Write out each of the following amounts.

Example: $25.30 Twenty-five dollars and thirty cents

1. $35.99 ____________________
2. $315.00 ____________________
3. $9.11 ____________________
4. $57.90 ____________________
5. $50.00 ____________________

B. ***Directions:*** Fill out the check below. Charlotte needs to pay Peebles Department Store $87.83 for a winter coat. Use today's date.

Charlotte A. Marmo
4590 Tulip Drive
Elizabethtown, PA 17022
(717) 367-5555

788

__________ 19____ 78-463/340

PAY TO THE
ORDER OF ____________________ $ ________

____________________ DOLLARS

First National Bank

FOR ______________ ______________

⑈003332⑈ ⑆052000618⑆ 6265936⑈

C. ***Directions:*** Write these number words correctly.

1. Fourty-nine dollars no cents ____________________
2. Ninty-nine dollars and three cents ____________________
3. Twelfe dollars and eleven cents ____________________
4. Eighten dollars and nine cents ____________________

Unit 12
Words to Watch

HOMONYMS: Words That Sound the Same

Probably the most commonly mixed-up words in English are those words that sound the same but have different meanings and different spellings. These words are called *homonyms*.

Examples: **there** — There goes George.
their — Their new car is nice.
they're — They're leaving in a few minutes.

Directions: Read the meanings of each pair of words. Then fill in the space in the sentence with the correct word.

weather — The general condition of the atmosphere at a certain time and place
whether — A word used to introduce an indirect question or an alternative

1. I don't know ____________ to go or not.
2. At the beach the ____________ was windy and warm.

past — A former time
passed — The past tense of the verb pass; went by; succeeded in

3. Yolanda was thrilled to find she had ____________ her math test.
4. In the ____________ Karen lived in Philadelphia.
5. Every morning on his way to school, Ronny ____________ by the ball field.

brake — Something that stops or slows the motion of something else
break — To separate into pieces

6. My good china will ____________ easily.
7. John's car skidded when he stepped on the ____________.

all ready — Completely prepared
already — Before; previously

8. Quinton has ____________ completed his math homework.
9. Are you ____________ for the party?

MORE HOMONYMS

Here are a few more of the most commonly used homonyms.

Directions: Read the meaning of each pair of words. Then fill in the space in the sentence with the correct word.

weak — Lacking in strength; not strong
week — Seven days; a unit of time

1. What do you have planned for this ________?
2. Joanie felt ________ after she had the flu.

principal — Main; most important
principal — The head of a school
principal — The amount of the debt for which you are charged interest; or the amount of money for which you are earning interest
principle — A rule of conduct; a basic truth or main fact

3. Only part of the car payment is ______________; the rest is interest.
4. Mrs. Francis was a popular ______________ at Somerset School.
5. The ______________ river of the United States is the Mississippi.
6. Don will never do anything against his ______________.

to — A preposition; for example, *to* in *to school.*
to — A word used to form the infinitive verb; for example, *to* in *to go.*
too — Very; also
two — A number; one more than one

7. Last night it was ________ cold and wet for our walk.
8. In ________ more days we will leave for our vacation.
9. Rickie wanted ________ learn to fly an airplane.
10. In the summer we usually walk ________ the pool.

hear — To receive a sound through the ears
here — This place

11. Bring the book over ________ please.
12. Excuse me, I can't quite ________ you.

through — In one side and out the other; among; from the beginning to the end of; completely to the end
threw — Caused to fly through the air

13. Mom! Judy ___________ away my papers again!
14. Are you ___________ with the dishes yet?

WORDS THAT SOUND ALMOST THE SAME

There are many words in English that sound almost like some other words. These pairs of words are easier to spell if you pronounce them correctly.

Directions: Read the definition. Say the words aloud. Fill in the spaces with the correct word.

probably — An *adverb* meaning "likely to happen"
probable — An *adjective* meaning "likely to happen"

1. Since Mike didn't know where he was going it was ______________ that he would get lost.
2. Since Mike doesn't know where he is going, he will ______________ get lost.

effect — The result; the influence something has on something else
affect — To produce a change in someone else; to influence

3. The weather does ____________ different people in different ways.
4. The ____________ of the weather on different people is different.

then — At that time; soon after
than — A word used to introduce a comparison.

5. John is taller ____________ his brother Ted.
6. We bought our ticket and ____________ saw the movie.

quiet — Still; calm; motionless
quite — Completely; entirely

7. The meeting did not start ____________ on time.
8. The night was so ____________ you could hear the stars twinkling.

advice — An opinion which someone gives to another about what to do
advise — To give someone your opinion about what they could or should do

9. Please give me some ____________ about what to do.
10. Please ____________ me about what to do.

choose — To pick out; to select (present tense)
chose — Picked out; selected (past tense)

11. The captain of the team ____________ the players. (past)
12. "Which dessert do you ____________?" asked the waiter. (present)

SOUND-ALIKE WORDS

We make mistakes with words that sound alike when we are in a hurry. "Take your time" is a good rule of thumb.

Directions: Read the definition. Say the words aloud. Fill in the spaces with the correct word.

later — The comparative form of *late*; something that happens after something else; after the usual time
latter — The second of two things or events
ladder — A device used for climbing

1. Randy seemed to arrive __________ every day.
2. "Bring the __________ over here," said the roofer.
3. Do you prefer the former or the __________?

formerly — In earlier times; in the past
formally — According to the rules; the opposite of *casually*

4. A business letter is written __________.
5. Our family __________ lived in Philadelphia.

accept — To receive willingly
except — Leaving out; other than

6. Fred decided to __________ the challenge.
7. Everyone __________ Sally arrived on time.

its — A possessive pronoun; *its* does not have an apostrophe (')
it's — A contraction of *it is*. The apostrophe replaces the letter which was left out.

8. The puppy whined because __________ bone was behind the sofa.
9. Where is __________ bone?
10. __________ behind the sofa.

whose — A possessive pronoun
who's — A contraction of *who is*

11. __________ that girl sitting behind Ralph?
12. I found a glove. Does anyone know __________ it is?

UNIT 12 REVIEW: Proofread, Edit, Revise

Directions: Replace each of the underlined words with another word that means nearly the same. Use a dictionary for help.

Diane looked out her window. She could hardly believe it, but there was a young female bald eagle in her front yard. The eagle was wounded. Because she was a veterinarian who specialized in the care of wildlife, Diane carefully approached the young bird. She talked softly. She moved slowly. She lifted the bird and carried her to the house. "We'll soon have you feeling better," she said.

Directions: Cross out every misspelled word. Write the correct word above it.

Diane called the City Zoo for advise. Soon, the young bald eagle found herself in a car rapidly traveling to the zoo, where their was a hospital. Diane didn't know weather the young creature would survive or not. They past a field where Diane saw another eagle. "Whose that?" she said out loud. "A friend of yours?" Diane thought the eagle seemed week. "Just hang in they're! Do you here?" Diane said too the bird.

ANSWER KEY

Page 5, Spelling Counts
Correct paragraph:

There are shoes today for every occasion. You can buy shoes especially for running or jogging. You can buy shoes especially made for walking. Every sport has its own special shoe. There are bowling, golfing, basketball, and baseball shoes in any athletic store. With all the shoes around, the most popular thing to do with shoes is still to take them off!

Page 6, Sentence Sense
Correct paragraph:

You can be a healthy person. You are in control of your life. You can eat healthy foods. When you are tired, you can rest or sleep. Everyday you can take a walk or do some other exercise. The choice of whether to smoke or not to smoke is yours. Perhaps most important of all, you can choose good friends. Doctors say that happy people are healthy people.

Page 7, Alive! Sentences!
A. 5 B. 4 C. 1
D. 3 E. 2
B. Correct paragraph:

When I arrived home from work last night, I was starving. What a shock to find that we were having repugnant liver for dinner! I would have preferred something succulent to eat, like a hamburger and french fries. Nevertheless, with nothing else to eat, and my stomach growling vociferously, I forced myself. Surprisingly enough, it didn't taste half bad. I guess when you're hungry, almost anything tastes satisfying.

Page 8, Write It Out! Contractions
A.

1.	a	8.	o
2.	a	9.	o
3.	a	10.	no
4.	woul	11.	o
5.	wi	12.	o
6.	i	13.	o
7.	wi	14.	o

B.

1.	he is	8.	they are
2.	we have	9.	they have
3.	can not	10.	should not
4.	do not	11.	I will
5.	you are	12.	it is
6.	I would	13.	you have
7.	she is	14.	would not

Page 9, Write It Out! Abbreviations
Correct paragraph:

Last **Monday**, Mrs. Cathy Young visited her **doctor**. His name is Rufus Webster. She hadn't seen Dr. Webster since the previous **October**. "I think you've gained two **pounds**," he said. Mrs. Young protested. "OK," he said. "It's one **pound** and thirteen **ounces**." "That's better," she said.

Page 10, Abbreviations
A. 1. 1700 B.C.
2. D.V.M.
3. Yes
4. 3 P.M.
5. Bachelor of Arts

B. 1. 1214 North Ellis Drive
2. 67 Park Avenue, Apartment 3A
3. 36 King Boulevard, Northeast
4. 3 Palmer Court

C. Answers will vary.

Page 11, Unit 1 Review
Correct paragraph:

How much snow is required for a major snowfall? What is a blizzard? It all depends on where you live, says Dr. Gamble. In Atlanta, Georgia, one inch is enough. In Minnesota, you would need several feet. A blizzard is a snowstorm with high winds. The wind blows the snow into huge piles called drifts. In a major blizzard, you will probably have to search around for your car or fence. People talk about a major snowfall for years afterward.

Page 12, Margins
A. Measurements are about:
Top: $\frac{1}{2}$ inch Left: $\frac{3}{4}$ inch
Right: 1 inch Bottom: $1\frac{1}{4}$ inches

B. Check for margins, indented paragraphs, and carefully formed letters.

Page 13, Neatness Counts
Check for carefully formed letters.

Page 14, Be Letter Perfect!
Check for accuracy and carefully formed letters.

Page 15, Unit 2 Review
Correct paragraph:

In some areas the weather turns cold in the winter. In those places, people enjoy the first day of spring very much! On that special day people wake up and look outside and see the sunshine. They see blue skies. They go outside to get the daily newspaper and feel the warmth in the air. It is truly a glorious feeling.

Page 16, Spelling Words Correctly
A. 1. all right
2. science
3. believe
4. friend
5. beginning

B. computer
family
writing
loves
misspelled
favorite

Page 17, Contractions
A.

1.	can't	11.	doesn't
2.	won't	12.	wouldn't
3.	didn't	13.	shouldn't
4.	I'll	14.	I'd
5.	I'm	15.	it's
6.	she's	16.	he's
7.	we'll	17.	we'd
8.	who's	18.	I've
9.	couldn't	19.	you're
10.	musn't	20.	she'll

B.

1.	he would	6.	will not
2.	she is	7.	you are
3.	who has	8.	we would
4.	I am	9.	I have
5.	we are	10.	does not

Page 18, Shortened Words
1. Callie Herman is a **junior** member of that law firm.
2. Jill Garman was born on **February** 21.
3. We would like you to come to dinner next **Thursday** evening
4. Karl, can you drive the dog to the **veterinarian**?
5. The kitten weighs one **pound** and seven **ounces**.
6. My bookmark is between **page** 34 and **page** 35.
7. Last week Sam bought a new **automobile.**

Page 19, More About Abbreviations
A. Answers will vary.
B.
1. Dr. Nancy Silvers
121 Van Ralston Street
Reading, Massachusetts 01867

2. Taylor and Wilson, Incorporated
12 West First Street, Southeast
Ocala, Florida 32674
3. Mrs. Elle Eshbaugh
18 West Hagerstown Drive
Montgomery, Alabama 36110

Page 20, Special Abbreviations
Sentences will vary.

Page 21, Last Name First!
A. Answers will vary.

B. Washington, Adams, Jefferson, Madison, Monroe

Page 22, First Name Last!
A. Answers will vary.

B. Check for capitalization and carefully formed letters.

Page 23, Street Addresses
Answers may vary. Some suggested definitions follow:
1. Drive — a road for cars
2. Turn — a short road, a bend in the road
3. Highway — a main road, a thoroughfare
4. Route — a road or course for traveling
5. Way — a road, street, or path
6. Park — a wooded area
7. Street — a public road in a town or city, especially a paved one
8. Boulevard — a broad, divided highway, often lined with trees
9. Turnpike — a toll road; especially one that is an expressway
10. Road — a way made for traveling

Page 24, City, State, and ZIP Code
A.

	Abbreviation	Full Word
1.	Mr.	Mister
2.	W.	West
3.	FL	Florida
4.	33062	
5.	Answers will vary.	
6.	Answers will vary.	
7.	C	
8.	A	

B.
9. Highway
10. Avenue
11. Northeast
12. Southwest
13. Mister
14. Doctor

Page 25, Unit 3 Review
A. Correct paragraph:
I would like to invite you to a party. It is a celebration of my birthday. You do not need to bring a present. I will be treating you!

B. Answers will vary.

C.
1. Federal Bureau of Investigation
2. American Federation of Labor-Congress of Industrial Organizations
3. United Nations International Children's Educational Fund
4. Unidentified Flying Object
5. Ultra High Frequency
6. Post Office Box

Page 26, Improving Spelling Skills
A. Correct paragraph:
At the ocean on Friday, we saw several ships passing by. They were on their way across the sea. One ship was stopping at Le Havre, a port in France.
I am planning to take a trip to France someday. I think I'll like being a world traveler.

B. a, e, i, o, u; Answers will vary.

Page 27, Recognizing Incorrect Spelling
1. especailly — especially
2. sacrafice — sacrifice
3. seperated — separated
4. famalies — families
5. peple — people
6. parde — parade
7. quikly — quickly
8. cheerring — cheering
9. afternon — afternoon

Page 28, Apostrophes: Possessives and Contractions
1. Possessive
2. Contraction
3. Contraction
4. Plural
5. Plural
6. Possessive
7. Plural
8. Possessive
9. Contraction
10. Possessive

Page 29, Vowels, Consonants, and Syllables
1. swim • ming
2. Skip • py
3. man • u • al
4. mug • gy
5. com • ma
6. mag • a • zine
7. run • ner
8. pen • cil
9. com • pu • ter
10. dic • tion • ar • y
11. swim • mer
12. Ma • ry
13. pa • per
14. neck • lace
15. pow • er
16. pur • ple
17. sharp • er
18. moun • tain
19. tel • e • vi • sion
20. rec • ord

Page 30, Doubling the Final Consonant

1.	batter	11.	jumping
2.	toaster	12.	topping
3.	playing	13.	slippery
4.	stepped	14.	clearing
5.	fitted	15.	swimmer
6.	planning	16.	cutting
7.	wrapped	17.	planted
8.	hemmed	18.	tapped
9.	hurting	19.	druggist
10.	begged	20.	running

Page 31, Words with Two Syllables
A.

1.	permitting	6.	equipped
2.	admitted	7.	forgetful
3.	traveler	8.	difference
4.	piloted	9.	beginning
5.	forgetting	10.	signaling

B.

1.	shopping	6.	regretful
2.	offered	7.	teacher
3.	nutty	8.	sitting
4.	batting	9.	opening
5.	wonderful	10.	laughing

Page 32, Words with a Final *E*
A.

1.	lovely	6.	writing
2.	writer	7.	lovable
3.	careful	8.	caring
4.	hopeless	9.	hoped
5.	lonely	10.	diving

B.

1.	practicing	11.	peaceable
2.	lonely	12.	excitement
3.	comparable	13.	believer
4.	useless	14.	wasted
5.	surprising	15.	arrangment
6.	changeable	16.	changing
7.	aging	17.	traveled
8.	circling	18.	advertisement
9.	argument	19.	voiced
10.	chasing	20.	proving

Page 33, I Before E
brief, friend, sleigh, shrieked, neighed, neighborhood, leisure, sleigh, weird, either

Page 34, Root Words

A.		*B.*	
a.	4	a.	5
b.	2	b.	3
c.	1	c.	2
d.	5	d.	1
e.	3	e.	4
	port; to carry		dict; to speak

1. A two-footed animal
2. A false name, such as a pen name that authors use.
3. The study of the mind

Page 35, Prefixes
A.

a.	3	e.	1
b.	7	f.	2
c.	6	g.	5
d.	4		

B.
1. extralegal
   Meaning: outside of the law
2. extraordinary
   Meaning: out of the ordinary
3. extrasensory
   Meaning: beyond the senses

Page 36. Negative Prefixes

A. a. 5
b. 3
c. 1
d. 2
e. 4
un; not, the opposite of

B. a. 5
b. 4
c. 1
d. 3
e. 2
in; the opposite of, not

C. a. 2
b. 4
c. 5
d. 3
e. 1
dis; not

Page 37, Suffixes

A. a. 3
b. 5
c. 1
d. 8
e. 2
f. 7
g. 6
h. 4
er, or, ist; one who

B. a. 3
b. 8
c. 6
d. 7
e. 1
f. 5
g. 2
h. 4
ness, ion, ment

Page 38, More Suffixes

A. 1. hopeful
2. meaningless
3. careful
4. thoughtless

B. a. 2
b. 5
c. 4
d. 3
e. 1

C.

1. enjoyable	5. colorful
2. socialize	6. biology
3. peaceable	7. beautify
4. actor	8. directions

Page 39, Unit 4 Review

Correct paragraph:

Won't you please come with me to the Ice Capades? The next show begins at 8 o'clock. I've got two tickets. Some of the skaters are very powerful. I'm just a beginner myself, but I like to skate, too. I use my friend Mary's skates since she outgrew them. She's my neighbor. I know you'll like the skating show as much as I do.

Page 40, Favorite Things

Answers will vary.

Page 41, Shopping for Groceries

A. Answers will vary, but the lists should include the following kinds of things:

loaf of bread, package of bacon, one dozen eggs, box of Cheerios, one-half gallon of milk, one-half gallon of orange juice, package of cheese, jar of mustard, bag of carrots, jar of applesauce, jar of pickles, lettuce, can of green beans, one pound of butter, bag of lemons, box of vanilla pudding mix, two lamb chops, rice

B. Answers will vary.

Page 42, Shopping at the Drugstore

A. Answers will vary. Some suggested responses are: cosmetics, dental floss, birthday cards, school supplies, etc.

B.

1. film	6. candy
2. tissues	7. dog food
3. magazine	8. envelopes
4. vitamins	9. birthday card
5. aspirin	10. scissors

C. Answers will vary. Check for spelling, accuracy, and appropriateness.

Page 43, A Week's Plan

Answers will vary. Check for spelling, accuracy, legibility, and appropriateness.

Page 44, Packing for Your Vacation

A. Answers will vary. Possible answers are: shirts, sweaters, dress shoes, underwear, toothbrush, toothpaste, socks, and jacket.

B. Answers will vary. Possible answers are: camera, film, books, magazines, games, deck of cards, stamps, pen, pencil, hairdryer, and binoculars.

Page 45, Planning a Party

A. Answers will vary. Check for spelling, accuracy.

B. Answers will vary. Check for spelling, handwriting, appropriateness.

Page 46, Homework and Other Projects

Answers will vary.

Page 47, Unit 5 Review

A. Answers will vary.
B. Check for accuracy.
C. Answers will vary.

Page 48, Putting Things in Order

Answers will vary. Suggested responses are:
1. alphabetical order
2. chronological order
3. by size
4. by color
5. by date
6. by subject

Page 49, Rules of Order

Practice 1:

Allen	Chinese
Fred	English
George	French
Jack	Polish
Richard	Russian

Practice 2:

July 17, 1979	897
August 20, 1980	1152
April 1, 1981	1401
January 3, 1983	1939
May 8, 1983	2012

Alphabetical by Title:
1. *Gone With the Wind*
2. *Huckleberry Finn*
3. *Lake Wobegon Days*
4. *Penrod*
5. *Watership Down*

By Date Published:
1. 1914
2. 1918
3. 1936
4. 1972
5. 1985

By Length:
1. 306
2. 337
3. 374
4. 429
5. 1037

Page 50, All Mixed Up

A.

List 1:	*List 2:*	*List 3:*
new	length	Barbie
nice	less	Beth
nine	letter	Bill
none	lift	Bob
now	long	Bunny

B.

List 1:	*List 2:*	*List 3:*
is	me	Jan
isn't	mean	Jane
it	meant	Jim
it'll	meat	Jimmy
its	meet	June

Page 51, Sorting Practice
A. Answers will vary.

B. Answers will vary.

Page 52, Numerical Order

A.
1. socks
2. cap
3. tee shirt
4. shorts
5. bathrobe
6. sweater
7. slacks
8. jacket
9. shoes

B.
1. cornmeal muffin
2. doughnut
3. French toast
4. roll
5. rye bread
6. white bread
7. Melba toast
8. pretzel

1. pretzel
2. Melba toast
3. white bread
4. rye bread
5. roll
6. French toast
7. doughnut
8. cornmeal muffin

Page 53, Unit 6 Review

A.
1. liver
2. sausage
3. frankfurter
4. chipped beef
5. hamburger
6. chicken
7. veal cutlet
8. turkey
9. pork

B.
1. *Black Beauty*
2. *Jane Eyre*
3. *Lad, a Dog*
4. *Lassie Come Home*
5. *Pride and Prejudice*
6. *Rebecca of Sunnybrook Farm*
7. *Tom Sawyer*
8. *Wuthering Heights*

1. *Pride and Prejudice*
2. *Jane Eyre*
3. *Wuthering Heights*
4. *Lassie Come Home*
5. *Black Beauty*
6. *Lad, a Dog*
7. *Tom Sawyer*
8. *Rebecca of Sunnybrook Farm*

Page 54, Getting from Here to There
1. Turn right on 4th Street.
2. Go four blocks.
3. Turn left on Wilson Blvd.
4. Turn left on Sara Place.
5. Look for the house on the right.

or

1. Go down Main Street.
2. Turn right on 5th Street. Go three blocks.
3. Turn left on Sara Place.
4. Go one block. Look for the house on the left.

Page 55, Writing Directions
Answers will vary. Be sure to describe every turn clearly.

Page 56, Mapmaking
Answers will vary. Be sure to describe every turn.

Page 57, Recording Directions
Answers will vary. A possible response will be:
1. Go up Satt Street.
2. Cross Wheeling Road.
3. Cross Rose Drive.
4. Turn left on Rolling Lane.
5. Look for the house on the right.

Page 58, Unit 7 Review
1. Correct
2. Turn left on Rt. 70. Go three blocks and turn right at Till Court.
3. Go one block and turn left on Rose Lane. Cross one road (the second part of Till Court). Anna's house is at the end of Rose Lane.

Page 59, Recognizing Sentences

A.
1. No
2. Yes
3. Yes
4. No
5. No
6. Yes

B. *Correct paragraph:*

In the eighteenth century, James Watt was working on the steam engine. That invention revolutionized travel. In the twentieth century, engineers and scientists are working on space travel. Do you think you will ever travel in space? That certainly would be exciting.

Page 60, Beginning a Sentence

A.
1. Start your sentence with a capital letter, please.
2. An Apple is a type of computer.
3. Wipe the mud off your shoes, Sammy. Thanks.
4. Did anyone see the pencil with my name on it?
5. The postal carrier usually comes about one o'clock.

B.

In the morning at five o'clock, the alarm clock rings. It is really too early for anyone to wake up. Don't you agree? I have a clock radio. I listen to music for a while. Finally, I have to get up. Wow! What a drag!

Page 61, Ending a Sentence
1. Exclamatory, !
2. Request, .
3. Statement, .
4. Statement, .
5. Question, ?
6. Request, .
7. Exclamatory, !
8. Question, ?
9. Statement, .
10. Statement, .

Page 62, Compound Sentences

A.
1. Wrong. Jerry and Sue like tennis. They play as often as they can.
2. Wrong. Write in complete sentences, and your grades will improve.
3. Right
4. Wrong. Last night Tom read his book several hours. Today he is sleepy.

B.
1. Jay plays basketball, **and** he hopes his team will win the championship.
2. Bill and Ralph met at the gym, **and** they both lifted weights.

Page 63, Unit 8 Review
Correct paragraph:

In the spring Chris decided to play soccer. Her new team practiced every Tuesday and Thursday afternoons. They met at Spring Lake Sports Park. Have you ever heard of it? This park was built by the city government for the people to use. Her coaches decided Chris would be a good goalie. She was very happy because that was her favorite position.

Page 64, Is It Complete?
1. Time and date of the message and more information are missing.
2. Time and date of the message are missing.
3. Time and date of the message are missing.
4. The name of the person who called, time and date of the message are missing.

Page 65, Messages at Home

A. Answers will vary. A possible response will be:

Mom, Christy is still at band practice. Please pick her up at 5 P.M. Love, Janet

B. Answers will vary.

Page 66, Recording Homework Assignments
Answers will vary.

Page 67, Messages at Work

To Mr. Jones
Date March 3 Time 3 P.M.

WHILE YOU WERE OUT

M Janet
of
Phone 555-3423
Area Code Number Extension

TELEPHONED		PLEASE CALL	X
CALLED TO SEE YOU		WILL CALL AGAIN	
WANTS TO SEE YOU		URGENT	
RETURNED YOUR CALL			

Message
Operator

To Mr. Lee
Date Time

WHILE YOU WERE OUT

M Mrs. Johnson
of
Phone
Area Code Number Extension

TELEPHONED		PLEASE CALL	
CALLED TO SEE YOU	X	WILL CALL AGAIN	
WANTS TO SEE YOU		URGENT	
RETURNED YOUR CALL			

Message Mrs. Johnson wants to order a dozen roses. Send them to her house on Friday, March 12.
Operator

Page 68, Ads and Announcements

A. Answers will vary. Check for spelling and complete sentences.

B. Responses will vary. Check for spelling, sentence structure, and content. The announcement should include the date, time, and place.

Page 69, Writing Ads

A. Responses will vary.

B. Responses will vary.

Page 70, Kinds of Letters

A. 5
B. 3
C. 2
D. 1
E. 4

Page 71, A Thank-You Note

Answers will vary.

Page 72, Invitations

The invitation should include the time, date, and place of the party. Students may write R.S.V.P. at the bottom instead of the last sentence. A possible response will be:

Dear Fred,

I am having a party at my home on Saturday, May 10 from 8:00 P.M. until midnight. Please bring potato chips and sodas. Let me know if you can come.

Sincerely,

Joe

Page 73, Addressing an Envelope

1. Valerie Brown
   1231 Santa Anna Parkway
   San Jose, CA 95129
2. Bob Aleshire
   1231 Johnson Drive, Apt. 3A
   Grifton, NC 28530
3. Johnny Kochert
   6034 Heatherwood Drive
   Alexandria, VA 22150
4. Joanie Matthews
   21234 Dawson Street, Apt. 2
   Juneau, Alaska 99801
5. Roy Theuret
   12 Howard Place
   Erie, PA 16510

Page 74, Parts of a Business Letter

A. Heading
B. Date
C. Inside Address
D. Salutation
E. Body
F. Complimentary Close
G. Signature
H. Typed Name and Title

Page 75, A Letter of Application

Responses will vary. Check letter against the sample on page 74. Check envelope with the sample on page 73.

Page 76, Special Kinds of Letters

Responses will vary.

Page 77, Unit 10 Review

Note to the teacher: Make sure the students use an appropriate greeting and close.

2121 Howard Road
Flint, Michigan 48504
April 3, 19___

George Wilson & Sons
Realty Company
1213 Superior Lane
Flint, Michigan 48504

Dear Mr. Wilson:

As we discussed on the telephone, I'd like you to sell our house. We hope to move from the area within the next two months. The price of the house will include the rugs, all appliances, and the drapes and curtains. We are having the house painted as you suggested. That should be finished this week.

Sincerely yours,
Fred Jackson
Fred Jackson

Page 78, Filling Out an Order Form

A. Responses will vary.

B. Students should be directed to answer the question as it applies to them.

Page 79, The Job Application

Responses will vary. Each space on the form should be completed. Use N/A in spaces when questions do not apply. Responses should be printed legibly.

Page 80, Job Application: Educational Background

Responses will vary.

Page 81, Job Application: Work Experience

Responses will vary.

Page 82, Job Application: References

A. Responses will vary.

B. 1. supervisor, reference
2. available, position
3. salary
4. single
5. dependents

Page 83, Abbreviations on Forms

A. Responses will vary.

B.
1. Bank Account Number
2. Post Office Box 34
3. Social Security Number
4. Apartment 101
5. 249-1330, Extension 34

Page 84, Writing Checks

A. 1. 786
2. May 3, 1989
3. Suburban Furniture
4. $125.35
5. Lamps
6. Charlotte A. Marmo

B. Note to the teacher: Direct students to complete the check. It should be payable to the Electric Company for $47.04.

Page 85, Number Words on Checks

A.
1. Thirty-five dollars and ninety-nine cents
2. Three hundred fifteen dollars and no cents
3. Nine dollars and eleven cents
4. Fifty-seven dollars and ninety cents
5. Fifty dollars and no cents

B. Note to the teacher: Direct students to complete the check. It should be payable to Peebles Department Store for $87.83. The purchase is a winter coat. Students should use the current date.

C.

1. Forty-nine dollars and no cents
2. Ninety-nine dollars and three cents
3. Twelve dollars and eleven cents
4. Eighteen dollars and nine cents

Page 86, Homonyms: Words That Sound the Same

1. whether
2. weather
3. passed
4. past
5. passed
6. break
7. brake
8. already
9. all ready

Page 87, More Homonyms

1. week
2. weak
3. principal
4. principal
5. principal
6. principle
7. too
8. two
9. to
10. to
11. here
12. hear
13. threw
14. through

Page 88, Words That Sound Almost the Same

1. probable
2. probably
3. affect
4. effect
5. than
6. then
7. quite
8. quiet
9. advice
10. advise
11. chose
12. choose

Page 89, Sound-Alike Words

1. later
2. ladder
3. latter
4. formally
5. formerly
6. accept
7. except
8. its
9. its
10. It's
11. Who's
12. whose

Page 90, Unit 12 Review

A. Answers will vary.

B. advise — advice
their — there
weather — whether
past — passed
Whose — Who's
week — weak
they're — there
here — hear
too — to